Collector Steiff® Values

Complete Guide
American Limited Editions
Animal Kingdom
1980-1990

by Peter Consalvi, Sr.
Research by Lisa DeMarco

Published by Hobby House Press

Hobby House Press, Inc.
Grantsville, Maryland 21536

A Very Special Dedication...

To my daughter, Lisa DeMarco, for all the hours of time in assembling and inputting years of material.

Front Cover: (Left) Anniversary Limited Edition, Mother/Baby, 0155/38, L.E. 7500 pieces, 1981-1982, $585. (Middle) Elephant on Wheels with Circus Calliope, 0100/86, L.E., 1986-1988, $1320. (Right) 100th Anniversary, Original Teddy, "Papa," 0153/43, L.E., 1980-1981, $935.

Frontispiece: (Left) Anniversary L.E., Mother/Baby, 0155/38, 1981-1982, $585. (Right) 100th Anniversary L.E. Original Teddy, "Papa," 0153/43, 1980, $935.

Title Page: (Left to Right) Circus Cage with Lying Lion, 0100/87, 1987, $605; Elephant on Wheels with Circus Calliope, 0100/86, 1986-1988, $1320.

Additional copies of this book may be purchased at $19.95
from
HOBBY HOUSE PRESS, INC.
1 Corporate Drive
Grantsville, Maryland 21536
or Call 1-800-554-1447
Please add $5.50 per copy for postage.
Or order from your favorite bookstore or dealer.

Photograph Credits:
Photographs of Steiff collectibles unless otherwise credited belong to the collections of Peter and Margaret Consalvi or Gary and Mary Ruddell.

Book Credits:
Photography: Tom Weigand Inc., Reading, Pennsylvania
Front Cover Photography: Karen A. Skidmore, KAS Studio, Frostburg, Maryland
Research: Lisa DeMarco
Introductory Text & Editing: Mary Beth Ruddell
Typesetting & Design: Margot Skelley
Layout & Design: Aimee Ruddell
Color Separations: Spectrum Co., Mount Laurel, New Jersey
Film: General Graphics, Inc., Cresaptown, Maryland
Printing & Binding: Friesen Printers, Altona, Manitoba, Canada

Table of Contents

Why I Decided to Do This Book 6

How to Use This Book 7

Collectibility of Steiff 8-9

Teddy Bears 10-47

Special Editions 48-49

Special Steiff® Collectibles 50-51

Rabbits 52-56

Cats 57-59

Dogs 60-62

Farmyard Animals 63-67

Woodland Animals 68-75

Characters 76-79

Animals of the Wild 80-88

Numerical Listing 89-111

100th Anniversary L.E. Original Teddy, 0153/43, 1980, $935.   Anniversary L.E. Mother/Baby (Mother's face shown), 0155/38, 1981, $585.

Why I Decided to Do This Price Guide

As a salesman for the Reeves Company not only did I sell Margarete Steiff animals, but I also helped merchants with in-store Steiff promotions. At every promotion I was asked by collectors, "What is my discontinued Steiff worth?" Collectors also sent me long lists of Steiff animals wanting to know values for insurance purposes and for their own knowledge. Even merchants would call me seeking valuing information to answer questions posed by collectors. Indeed there are price guides, such as the *4th Teddy Bear and friends® Price Guide* by Linda Mullins and *Contemporary Teddy Bear Price Guide: Artists to Manufacturer* by Terry & Doris Michaud, which provide this type of information. Although these are excellent price guides, the books do not focus exclusively on Steiff made during the 1980s with the depth required to answer questions posed by the contemporary Steiff teddy bear and animal collector. My research, photographs and values are dedicated to the Steiff collector who loves the 1980-1990 era. Using my book, *Collector Steiff Values*, everyone can quickly identify when their animal was made, for how long it was produced, what the animal originally sold for, and its most recent collector value.

Antidotal Steiff Stories

There Just Ain't More Moe's!

As I was waiting for a merchant to finish with his customer, I overheard the following exchange. The merchant, "You should buy one of these Steiff animals, they are rare." The customer asked why the Steiff's were expensive compared with other manufacturer's animals. The merchant stated, "You see these Steiff animals are made of 'moe' hair and the 'moe's' are becoming extinct in Germany." "Frankly there just ain't more 'moe's'!" he exclaimed. The customer bought the Steiff animal. I asked the merchant after the customer had left, "Why did you say 'moe's'?" His answer was that he had no idea about why the Steiff animals were so expensive, but he thought it sounded like a good idea at the time.

Special Steiff animals are made from mohair. Mohair is a fabric or yarn made wholly or in part of the long silk hair of the Angora goat. I am happy to report that the Angora goat is not on the endangered animals list. Mohair has become even more expensive since the 1980s and animals made from mohair will naturally become even pricer.

Stories continued page 9

"The Teddy Tea Party," 0204/16, 1982, $385.

How to Use This Book

First please read all introductory text so that you will know what collectors look for to identify, date and value their Steiff animals. I have undertaken this book, *Collector Steiff Values*, to make the user of the book an appraiser and to give them the data from which to identify, date, deduce important production information such as manufacturers suggested retail and the most recent collector value.

Organization of the Book

To aid the reader the book is divided into sections. The first section has the animals organized into type as many collect by their favorite animals. Each sectional listing has the data organized in numerical tag number order from smallest to largest. All animals produced by Steiff fall into one of the types: Teddy Bears, Rabbits, Cats, Dogs, Farmyard Animals, Woodland Animals, Animals of the Wild, Characters or Special Collectibles (such as the Circus Wagons). A collector can see what they have in their collections and what they must need.

Should the reader want a quick reference and has the tag number they can refer to the last twenty-two pages which has a listing of all the Steiff production sold in America from 1980 through 1990 from the smallest tag number to the largest tag number.

How to Read an Entry from the Tables

Reading from left to right:

The Number corresponds to the number on the tag of the animal or set. The numbers after the slash refer to the metric size. The metric size measures the distance from either the bottom to the top of the animal or from the nose to the tail of the animal. The use of "00" signifies that this is a set of animals.

The Description may include the name of the animal; the description of the animal: including color, position of animal, whether part of a set, etc.; the abbreviations of LE means limited edition and mhr means made from mohair.

The Year and Amount Go across the entry until you come to the amount. This figure represents the suggested selling price to the consumer and reading up would tell the year of issue. Each ensuing price under each year would indicate the suggested selling price for that year. The last entry would signify that the animal was discontinued during that year by the manufacturer. Note: Because the book's coverage concludes with 1990, a price in the 1990 column could indicate either an animal was introduced in 1990 with the suggested selling price or if the animal was discontinued before 1990 a collectors value.

The Collectibility of Steiff

Steiff has been making bears and other related animals for over one hundred years but it was the 1980s when Steiff would have their full impact on the American collecting world. Experts feel that this is due to the enthusiasm Steiff created with their 100th Anniversary Limited Edition "Papa" Bear (0153/43) released in 1980. Steiff had been creating playthings for 99 years when the unique event of how to celebrate the 100th anniversary of their first plaything dictated something special. The Papa Bear or 100th Anniversary Edition saw 11,000 created worldwide, 6,000 for Germany (with the certificate in German) and 5,000 for the United States (with the certificate in English). With this bear Steiff began a decade of releasing classic limited edition replica bears and animals (Museum Replicas or Editions).

Papa effected the public better than Steiff even expected. Dick Frantz, salesman for Steiff U.S.A. Ltd., was surprised at how well Papa was received. He knew that releasing a Steiff anniversary bear in the United States was a good venture, but he never thought it would have the impact that it did. Papa was ordered by retail stores and eagerly bought by collectors before he was even placed on the shelf. The next year Steiff released the Mother and Baby (0155/38) as part of the Papa series and the enthusiasm grew.

With the production of the Papa Bear Steiff rekindled the love for the teddy bear in the general public. Papa was produced with the same quality as the original and stuffed with excelsior. Excelsior was a popular stuffing material used by Steiff until 1972-1973. At this time some problems arose with the material. First, it was very difficult to work with because it required hand stuffing and took very strong men to perform the task. Then it also caused allergic reactions in some of the workers. It was abandoned as a stuffing because of those problems but Steiff reinitiated its use to produce the same quality bears as their early 1900s bears in 1980 and have been using it ever since.

The collectibility of Steiff is due largely to Steiff products being viewed as the ultimate in classic designs and depth of colors as well as to the quality and craftsmanship of their products. No company before Steiff has been able to produce replicas that are so similar to the original bears that there is absolutely no difference besides a little time. This is due to the time and energy Steiff takes to make an animal. Every piece of material is cut out by hand and sewn individually. The material is of the finest quality including mohair, trivara and an incredibly soft Molly fabric used for children's toys. According to Cynthia Britnall of Cynthia's Country Store, "Each bear is done with the best craftsmanship and material in the bear world. That is what makes them the best collectible on the market."

Steiff not only takes the time to perfect craftsmanship but they take the time to add realism to each piece with airbrushing techniques. This detail has separated them from any other plush company. The amount of airbrushing used on an animal varies. Sometimes it is used for shadow purposes and sometimes it is used for detail spots on a giraffe. Whatever the case, the airbrushing adds realistic detail to every creation.

During the 1980 decade, the demand for limited editions was high among collectors and the sales in this market skyrocketed. Specialty bear shops emerged to meet this demand, and Steiff animals and bears were available in antique shops, collector shops, toy stores, gift shops, doll shops, mail order and appearing at collector shows throughout the United States. Steiff had a fantastic advertising strategy in 1980 that lead them to a great American market.

Value

The value of a Steiff Collectible is determined in a variety of ways. The sophisticated collector is looking for a mint-in-box animal with all its tags, certificate and original box. These items are often hard to find because not all animals have a certificate or special box.

Some of the important factors in determining a price are:
1. The color of the tag on the animal. There are two colors that are used — white and yellow. The white tag signifies a limited edition animal. These animals are more expensive and their current price and investment potential are determined by the number produced and demand by collectors.

The yellow tag means that Steiff has the right to reintroduce a line. An animal with a yellow tag is not limited to a certain number manufactured or time table of production.
2. The number of pieces of an animal manufactured. This is usually determined by the color of the tag but that does not always hold true. Some yellow tag bears have become more popular and are in higher demand than some white tag bears. The most important distinguishing factor a collector is looking for is the color, the cut and the uniqueness of the bear.
3. Special Edition Bears. These include special editions made for stores like Mr. Vanilla of Hobby Center Toys and the bears made especially for the Walt Disney World® and Disneyland Teddy Bear Conventions.
4. Condition. The mint condition animal has the original box, ear tag, chest tag, certificate and occasionally the packaging carton. White tag bears were primarily boxed but some bears do not have a box. Boxed sets did not come with a certificate. In the early years of white tag manufacturing the number of the edition was listed only on the certificate. Later this number was also placed on the ear tag.

Grading

"Mint Condition" is the highest grading any animal can receive. In order to have "mint condition" the animal must have all original tags, original box and must be unsoiled. These bears are hardly ever removed from the box.

A piece may be graded "Excellent Condition" with no box, no breast tag, limited edition certificate missing, but generally very clean, new condition.

Grading from this point on is "Very Good" slightly soiled, "Good" slightly worn, "Fair" soiled and worn, "Poor" soiled, badly worn and mold odor.

The Museum Series

In 1980 Steiff opened a museum in the first Steiff factory building in Giengen, Germany to celebrate 100 years of making playthings. This museum highlights every piece ever made by Steiff in a chronological presentation. It includes animals in mint condition as well as some animated displays.

The Museum Series produced in the 1980s are exact replicas of the earlier pieces. These pieces happen to consist mainly of other animals besides bears although some action bears (a bear on four wheels or a roly poly bear) are considered part of this series.

Museum pieces come in a silver box with no certificate and a numbered ear tag. They were not limited to a certain number in the beginning but were marked as a number but not marked as are limited editions out of the edition number. Limited edition numbers are given now.

Included in the Museum Series are larger pieces called Studio pieces. These Studio pieces "accomplish styling combined with the best materials and handicraft ability to produce large true-to-nature imitations of animals."

Special Editions

This book would not be complete without information about special Steiff editions. These special editions are most interesting to collectors because of their limited distribution and scarcity as well as the unique influence such partnerships add to the Steiff design. The focus of this book are the American editions.

German Editions. From the first collector's edition, the Papa Bear has sprung others such as the 1988 *Teddy Baby and the Wolf* created for the Wolf Toy Store in Geingen. This unique white Teddy Baby saw 1000 produced and its original sell-out offering at $200 has now increased in value to $650 on the collectors' market.

United Kingdom. Collectors also covet the usual 2000 to 3000 teddy bear editions produced for collectors in the British Isles. Harrod's, Hamley's and Teddy Bears of Whitney (Alfonzo) have all produced special editions.

United States Special Editions. Suzanne Gibson Dolls made and distributed by Reeves International (who also distributed Steiff in the 1980s) also offered some special sets combining a Suzanne Gibson Doll with Steiff animals. 16" Suzanne Gibson Goldilocks (#4003 from 1984-85) with Three Steiff Bears (25cm boy bear, 30cm mother bear, and 32cm father bear); 8" Suzanne Gibson Goldilocks (#4004 from 1985-86) with Three Steiff Bears (14cm boy bear, 18cm mother bear, and 22cm father bear); and a Suzanne Gibson Alice (#4005 from 1986-87), a limited edition of 3000 pieces, with Steiff animals (13cm cat, 13cm mouse, and 20cm Rabbit with big pocket watch).

1989 Ronald McDonald Dickie. 100 Dickie Bears were dressed in Ronald McDonald Clown Outfits. They were sold to benefit the Ronald McDonald House.

Walt Disney Conventions

Walt Disney World and Disneyland Conventions have lead the boom in teddy bear collecting. These conventions, the first being in Walt Disney World in 1988, highlighted specific artists and their bears. "These conventions sparked the worldwide interest in bears," says Cynthia Britnall of Cynthia's Country Store. The Steiff bears produced for Disney conventions were especially valuable because they were a collector piece for both the bear and Disney enthusiast.

Some special editions include the 1991 Walt Disney World® Mickey Mouse Bear. This bear had a Mickey Mouse Masque and a Mickey head outline Steiff pin. The following year a similar Minnie Mouse was produced.

The Disneyland conventions (1992 and 1993) had some pretty popular bears produced. Two of these bears have escalated quite dramatically in value as they are larger bears produced in small quantities. These bears came in two sizes and played music. The smaller bear played "When You Wish Upon a Star" while the larger bear played "When You Wish Upon a Star" and "It's a Small World After All."

Antidotal Steiff Stories continued

Mr. Steiff, Your Name is "Steeef"

A German Company carrying a German family name often puzzles the American as to its proper pronunciation, sometimes to humorous ends. While helping Mr. and Mrs. Hans Otto Steiff at a Baltimore Teddy Bear show, I witnessed such an encounter. A very determined woman walked up to the table where Mr. Steiff was signing Steiff animals and with a bold, superior tone advised Mr. Steiff that the correct pronunciation of his name was "Steeef." Mr. Steiff looked at me then looked back at the woman and said with a smile, "Madame I don't care if you call me Steiff, Steeef, or Stiff as long as you like our stuffed animals. It is okay with me!"

Editor's Note: The correct pronunciation is (phonetically) "Shh-tife."

This classic design set the tone for the 1980s, 100th Anniversary L.E. Original Teddy Bear, "Papa," 0153/43, 1980, $935. German edition 6000 pieces, English edition 5000 pieces.
Opposite Page: Anniversary L.E. Mother/Baby, 0155/38, 1981, $585.

Bears

Bears

Teddy Bears

Steiff #	Description	80-81	81-82	82-83	83-84	84-85	85-86	86	87	88	89	90	Current
0082/20	Roly Poly Bear, 1894, 2 yr LE					69	70	70	70	80	80	95	105
0085/12	Bear on Wheels, LE 12,000						95	100	100	120	120	165	182
0090/11	Polar Bear Jntd Legs/Rtng Head, LE 3000								95	95		155	265
0115/18	Roly Poly Bear w/Rattle 1908, mhr, LE									125	125	125	138
0116/25	Record Teddy, 1913, LE 4000											300	330
0120/19	Bear Band Leader w/Baton, LE									125	125	135	149
0130/28	Bear on 4 Legs, Univ. Head Mov., mhr, LE 4000										400	400	465
0131/00	Three Bears in a Tub, LE 1800								275	275		310	375
0132/24	"Wiwag" Seesaw P-Toy w/Two Bears, mhr, LE									260	260	260	286
0135/20	Baby Bear Pull Toy, cover w/mhr, LE 4000										275	275	303
0150/32	Richard Steiff 1902-1903 Bear, LE				90	100						285	350
0151/25	1904 Cinnamon Bear, mhr, LE					70	75	79				165	190
0151/32	1904 Cinnamon Bear, mhr, LE					85	90	95				265	325
0151/40	1904 Cinnamon Bear, mhr, LE					125	135	145				435	525
0153/43	100th Annv. L.E. Original Teddy	150										800	935
0155/15	Baby Bear in Christening Outfit, LE							60	75	75		99	109
0155/22	Flower Bearer, L.E. 2000 pc.						75	80	100	100		125	140
0155/23	Ring Bearer, L.E. 2000 pc.						75	80	100	100		125	140
0155/26	Margaret Strong Bear, mhr, LE			48	48	50	53	56	69	100	100	100	110
0155/32	Margaret Strong Bear, mhr, LE			62	62	65	69	73	89	135	135	135	142
0155/34	Victorian Girl Bear 1986, LE 1200						125					225	248
0155/35	Victorian Boy Bear 1986, LE 1200						125	125				225	248
0155/36	Bride, L.E. 2000, 1984				100	110	125	150		200	200	215	241
0155/37	Groom, L.E. 2000, 1984				100	110	125	150		200	200	215	241
0155/38	Anniv. Ltd/Mother/Baby, mhr, 7500		150									495	585
0155/38	Santa Bear, 1000 pc., 1986							125	150	200	200	200	220
0155/42	Margaret Strong Bear, mhr, LE				90	95	100	105	125	200	200	200	240
0155/51	Margaret Strong Gold Bear, mhr, LE					185	195	205	250	350	350	350	389
0155/60	Margaret Strong Gold Bear, mhr, LE					250	285	300	375	495	495	495	549
0156/00	Margaret Strong Cinnamon Bear Set, mhr, LE					300	300					590	680
0156/26	Cinnamon Bear, mhr, LE							53				100	115
0156/32	Cinnamon Bear, mhr							69				135	155
0156/42	Cinnamon Bear, mhr, LE							100				195	224
0157/26	Margaret Strong Cream Bear, mhr, LE					50	53	56				145	161
0157/32	Margaret Strong Cream Bear, mhr, LE					65	69	73				185	205
0157/42	Margaret Strong Cream Bear, mhr, LE					95	100	105				265	294
0157/51	Margaret Strong Cream Bear, mhr, LE					195	205					565	625
0157/60	Margaret Strong Cream Bear, mhr, LE					285	300					625	975
0158/17	Snap-Apart Bear, mhr, LE 5000										135	275	325
0158/25	White Bear, Leather Paws, mhr, LE						60	60	60			165	195
0158/31	White Bear, Leather Paws, mhr, LE						79	79	79			255	325
0158/41	White Bear, Leather Paws, mhr, LE						110	110	110			325	438
0158/50	White Bear, Leather Paws, mhr, LE						225					1200	1535
0160/00	M. Strong Choc. Brown Set, 4 pc.				275							480	585
0162/00	"The Birthplace of the Teddy," LE, 1984					150	159	159	159			260	300
0163/19	Bear Drsd as Clown, White Tag								50			195	220
0163/19	Bear Drsd as Clown, Yellow Tag								50			125	155
0163/20	Clown Teddy, mhr, LE 5000										100	100	110
0164/29	Somersault Bear, mhr, LE 5000											395	410
0164/30	Odd Yellow Dolly Bear, 471 pc.								135			245	295
0165/28	1909 Gold Teddy, mhr, LE					55	59	62	62			75	100
0165/38	1909 Gold Teddy Bear, mhr, LE				80	85	90	95				110	165
0165/51	1909 Gold Teddy, mhr, LE					150	159	169				435	487
0165/60	1909 Gold Teddy, mhr, LE					275	290	290				580	680
0166/25	Blond Teddy, 1909, mhr, LE									100	100	100	109
0166/35	Blond Teddy, 1909, mhr, LE									145	145	145	160
0166/43	Blond Teddy, 1909, mhr, LE									225	225	225	248
0167/22	Giengen Bear, Grey, 1906 Rep, mhr, LE							55	69	100	100	100	109
0167/32	Giengen Bear, Grey, mhr, LE					85	90	100		160	160	160	176
0167/42	Giengen Bear, Grey, mhr, LE					120	125	150		225	225	225	350
0167/52	Giengen Bear, Grey, 1906 Rep, mhr, LE						195	250		350	350	350	500
0168/22	Giengen Bear, Beige, 1906 Rep, mhr, LE							55	69	100	100	100	109
0168/42	Giengen Bear, Beige, 1906 Rep, mhr, LE						125	150		225		235	259
0169/65	Teddy Bear, Grey/Brown Tipped, 1926, mhr, LE 5000											525	595
0170/32	Teddy Clown 1926 Rep, LE 10,000							150	150			395	435
0171/25	Teddy Rose, LE											195	235
0171/41	Teddy Rose w/Ctr. Seam, LE 10,000								200	300	230	345	350
0172/32	Dicky Bear, LE 20,000, 1985					100	105	105		125		225	275
0173/40	Black Bear, 1907 Rep, LE									300	300	600	535

Teddy Bears

Steiff #	Description	80-81	81-82	82-83	83-84	84-85	85-86	86	87	88	89	90	Current
0207/41	Original Teddy, Grey, mhr, LE							85	85	160	160	160	184
0208/10	Black Teddy Bear, mhr, LE				36		38	38				88	95
0208/14	Black Teddy Bear, mhr, LE						30					75	81
0209/12	Original Teddy, Black, mhr											50	54
0209/15	Original Teddy, Black, mhr											70	76
0210/12	Original Teddy, Blond, Mini-Mohair										50	50	54
0210/15	Original Teddy, Blond, Mini-Mohair										70	70	76
0210/22	Teddy Roosevelt Comm. Set, mhr, LE			200								275	325
0211/10	Original Teddy, Rose, LE 8000											60	64
0211/12	Original Teddy, Rose, mhr											50	54
0211/15	Original Teddy, Rose, mhr											70	76
0211/26	Luv Bear-er, mhr						45	48				135	151
0211/36	Luv Bear-er, mhr						60	64				175	196
0212/10	Original Teddy, Cream, mhr, LE							38	38			82	90
0213/10	Original Teddy, Cinnamon, mhr, LE							38	38			82	90
0214/10	Original Teddy, Gold, mhr, LE							38	38			82	90
0215/35	Dormy Bear	60	67	68	68							150	162
0217/34	Dorma Bear		65	66	66	66	66	70				145	149
0218/16	Bear		28	28	28	28						60	62
0220/30	Orsi Bear	48	54	55	55							120	130
0223/30	Bruno Bear, Jointed, mhr, LE			60	60	62	62	62				135	149
0224/35	Petsy Soft											93	100
0225/27	Baby Ophelia with Tutu, mhr, LE									140	140	140	154
0225/42	Ophelia Bear, Jointed, mhr, LE					150	159	169	200	275	275	275	320
0226/28	Growling Bear											100	107
0227/33	Schnuffy Bear Dressed, 1907 Rep, mhr, LE								200	275	275		303
0228/33	Growling Bear, mhr							90		125	125	125	137
0228/38	Growling Bear, mhr							125		165	165	165	182
0228/48	Growling Bear, mhr							195		250	250	250	275
0230/20	Teddy Petsy, Rust					39	39					69	74
0230/28	Teddy Petsy, Rust					50	50	53	64	95	95	63	68
0230/35	Teddy Petsy, Rust					70	70	75	90	130	130	85	92
0230/45	Teddy Petsy, Rust					100	100	105	140	190	190	120	130
0233/20	Teddy Petsy, Blonde					39	39	41	41			65	70
0233/28	Teddy Petsy, Blonde					50	50	53	65	95	95	63	68
0233/35	Teddy Petsy, Blonde					70	70	75	90	130	130	85	92
0233/45	Teddy Petsy, Blonde					100	100	105	140	190	190	120	130
0233/80	Teddy Petsy, Blonde						400	425	500	500		600	648
0235/20	Teddy Petsy, Cream					39	39	41	41			65	70
0235/28	Teddy Petsy, Cream					50	50	53	65	95	95	63	68
0235/35	Teddy Petsy, Cream					70	70	75	90	130	130	85	92
0235/45	Teddy Petsy, Cream					100	100	105	140	190	190	120	130
0236/28	Petsy Teddy, Augbergine											62	75
0237/20	S-Soft Teddy, Beige, Jointed, mhr, LE					40						90	97
0237/28	Petsy Teddy, Blackberry											62	75
0237/28	S-Soft Teddy, Beige, Jointed, mhr, LE					55	59	62	62			125	135
0237/35	S-Soft Teddy, Beige, Jointed, mhr, LE					75	79	85	85			165	178
0237/45	S-Soft Teddy, Beige, Jointed, mhr, LE					110	115	115	115			245	265
0238/35	Petsy Teddy											85	92
0240/28	Petsy Panda							60	72	110	110	68	73
0240/35	Petsy Panda							80	96	150	150	150	162
0240/45	Petsy Panda							115	140	200		200	216
0245/40	Passport Bear, mhr, LE						110	115	140	210		225	240
0251/34	Berlin Bear, mhr, LE						110	115	115			210	230
0255/35	Clifford Berryman Bear, mhr, LE							170	225	225			248
0270/28	Teddy Dressed as a Bride, mhr						100	125	175			180	198
0271/28	Teddy Dressed as a Groom, mhr						100	125				180	198
0275/28	Teddy Dressed with Dirndl, mhr						100	125	175			175	193
0276/28	Teddy Dressed with Lederhosen, mhr						100	125	175		175	175	193
0280/28	Teddy Dressed as a Sailor Boy, mhr						100	125	175		175	175	193
0281/28	Teddy Dressed as a Sailor Girl, mhr						100	125	175		175	175	193
0283/28	Teddy Dressed w/Black Forest Outfit, mhr								150	150		165	182
0284/28	Teddy Dressed w/Farmer Outfit, mhr								150	150		165	182
0290/32	Toddel	43	50	51								100	108
0302/30	Zotty	60	67	70	70	70	70					110	119
0302/40	Zotty	85	95	98	98	98	98					160	173
0302/50	Zotty	125	140	145	145	145	145	155				230	248
0305/22	Zotty	34	40	41								200	230
0305/30	Zotty Bear						63	67	81	135	135	85	92

Teddy Bears

Steiff #	Description	80-81	81-82	82-83	83-84	84-85	85-86	86	87	88	89	90	Current
0305/32	Zotty, mhr	46	50	55								270	311
0305/40	Zotty Bear						95	100	125	200	200	125	135
0305/45	Zotty, mhr	98	115	120								410	472
0305/50	Zotty Bear						130	140	170	250	250	150	162
0310/19	Buddha Bear, mhr				40	40	43					130	155
0312/30	Minky Zotty									135	135	89	96
0312/40	Minky Zotty									200	200	130	140
0312/50	Minky Zotty									250	250	155	167
0318/32	Molly Minky										115	77	83
0318/42	Molly Minky										160	160	173
0320/55	Molly Teddy		115	120								230	248
0320/65	Molly Teddy		160	165	165	165	165	175	210	265	265	165	178
0321/22	Molly Teddy, Champagne									65	65	42	45
0321/32	Molly Teddy, Champagne									115	115	70	76
0321/55	Molly Teddy, Champagne			100	100	100	105	140		200	200	125	138
0322/22	Molly Teddy, Cream									65	65	42	45
0322/32	Molly Teddy, Cream									115	115	70	74
0322/40	Molly Teddy, Cream				80	80	85	110		150	150	96	104
0323/50	Super Molly Teddy, Standing								395	525		539	582
0323/60	Molly Teddy, Brown											175	189
0323/65	Molly Panda		158	165	165							295	319
0324/60	Super Molly Teddy, Lying								395	525		525	567
0324/75	Molly Teddy											265	286
0326/32	Molly Panda, B/W	52	58	60	60	60	60	65	78	110	110	110	121
0326/45	Molly Panda, B/W	93	100	110	110	110	110	115	140	190		190	209
0327/32	Molly Panda, Brown	48	54									130	143
0327/45	Molly Panda, Brown	90	100									220	242
0327/85	Standing Bear on 4 Legs								2963		4335	3895	3995
0328/99	Bear Standing on 2 Legs								2963		4335	3895	3995
0329/08	Brown Bear Standing on 4 Legs								2315			2500	2900
0329/16	Brown Bear Standing								2315			2500	2900
0330/32	Molly Bear	36	40	41	41	45	45	48	58	95	95	95	105

Margaret Strong Bear, 0155/32, L.E., 1983 on, $142.

Teddy Bears

Steiff #	Description	80-81	81-82	82-83	83-84	84-85	85-86	86	87	88	89	90	Current
0330/45	Molly Bear	84	97	100	100	100	100	105	125	160		175	193
0330/70	Molly Bear	190	250	265	265	265						410	451
0331/22	Molly Koala	37	40									76	84
0331/33	Molly Bear, Sitting									185	185	185	200
0331/40	Molly Koala	68	68									125	138
0332/45	Molly Petsy		95	98	98	98						180	194
0333/35	Molly Grizzly		95	98	98							180	194
0333/55	Molly Grizzly		170	175								330	356
0334/45	Molly Polar Bear		95	98	98							180	194
0334/55	Molly Polar Bear		140	145								270	292
0341/40	Super Molly Bear				90	90	90	95	125	170	170	170	187
0341/65	Super Molly Bear				185	185	185	195	250	350	350	350	385
0341/90	Super Molly Bear				300	300	300	320	3100	600	600	600	660
0341/98	Super Molly Bear				450	450	450	475	575			785	864
0341/99	Super Molly Bear	600	680	700	700							920	1012
0343/25	Molly Bear									150		97	105
0343/32	Molly Bear									220		145	157
0343/40	Molly Bear									325		205	221
0345/35	Molly Bear									205		135	146
0345/45	Molly Bear									290		185	200
0345/60	Molly Bear									350		230	248
0345/80	Molly Bear										575	375	405
0347/55	Molly Bear, Brown											165	178
0355/35	Molly Polar Bear, Sitting											135	146
0380/28	Baloo Bear	46	51									225	248
0409/19	Bear, Standing St 69"	2493	2593									4700	4800
0410/50	Bear on Wheels	200										685	754
0417/60	Brown Bear Cub		175	180	180							340	367
0438/70	Super Molly Panda						195	205	250			320	346
0438/98	Super Molly Panda						425	450	450			695	751

Teddy Roosevelt Commemorative Set, 0210/22, L.E., 1983-1984, $325.

Teddy Bears

Steiff #	Description	80-81	81-82	82-83	83-84	84-85	85-86	86	87	88	89	90	Current
0439/07	Panda				150							225	239
0439/13	Panda				425							575	610
0467/23	Polar Bear, White	50	57	58								95	105
0468/60	Polar Bear Cub		175	180	180							340	367
0470/99	Polar Bear			2565	2565							4600	4700
0472/99	Polar Bear			945	945	945	945	1195			1843	1700	1800
0477/60	Panda Bear Cub		188	195	195							345	373
1210/25	Bear, Standing											81	87
1212/25	Bear, Sitting											89	96
1215/25	Bear, Lying											89	96
1220/25	Polar Bear, Standing											81	87
1222/25	Polar Bear, Sitting											89	96
1225/25	Polar Bear, Lying											89	96
1444/12	Browny Bear						23	24	30	50	50	32	35
1445/12	Browny Bear	17	20	21	23	29						42	46
1446/11	Koala Bear		22	23	23	23	23	25	30	42	42	45	49
1447/17	Polar Bear		25	26	26							50	54
2877/30	Jr. Petsy			74	74	74						130	140
2920/16	Snuffy Bear				29	29	29	31	38			50	54
2921/16	Snuffy Bear								42	56		60	65
3490/45	Mimic Bear				75	75	75	79	95			165	178
5030/17	Pummy Bear										90	90	97
5030/21	Pummy Bear										115	115	124

Museum Editions.
Left: Felt Elephant, Replica 1880, 0080/08, L.E., 1984-1989, $83.
Middle: Roly Poly Bear, Replica 1894, 0082/20, L.E., 1984-1989, $105.
Right: Bear on Wheels, 0085/12, L.E., 12,000 pieces, 1985-1989. $182.

Teddy Bears

Steiff #	Description	80-81	81-82	82-83	83-84	84-85	85-86	86	87	88	89	90	Current
5035/17	Pummy Koala Bear										105	105	113
5035/21	Pummy Koala Bear										140	80	86
5352/33	Cosy Bear									110		110	119
5353/25	Cosy Bear, Honey Gold			53	53							95	103
5354/25	Cosy Bear, Dk. Brown			53	53							65	70
5355/26	Cosy Bear		35	35	35	35	35	37	45			95	103
5355/36	Cosy Bear		55	55	55	55	55	58	70			95	103
5357/25	Cosy Panda					67	67	70	90	120		120	130
5358/18	Cosy Koala							45	55	80		80	86
5358/27	Cosy Koala			58	58	58	58					95	103
5358/28	Cosy Koala							70	85	125		125	135
5358/38	Cosy Koala							100	125			160	173
5358/50	Cosy Koala							200	250			320	346
5405/17	Cosy Polar Bear					35	35	37	47	47		47	51
5405/30	Cosy Polar Bear				50	50	50	53	64	95	95	95	103
5505/25	Cuddly Bear			50	50							95	103
5600/18	Floppy Bear				36	36	36	38	48	65		65	70
5600/25	Floppy Bear				50	50	50					95	103
5651/16	Mini Floppy Bear										50	50	54
5652/16	Min Floppy Polar Bear										50	50	54
5700/20	Teddy	39	43	43								85	94
5700/30	Teddy	57	62	62								120	132
5701/22	Kiddi Bear										75	75	81
5702/20	Kiddi Bear										75	75	81
5750/22	Drolly Bear											52	56
6242/20	Toldi Bear			25	28							48	52
6242/30	Toldi Bear			49	53	53						90	97
6270/27	Toldi Bear									80		80	86
6461/27	Bear (Hand Puppet)	26	28	28	28	28	28	30	36			60	67
6485/32	Happy Bear										95	95	103
6560/17	Teddy (Hand Puppet), mhr	19										110	123

Left: "Wiwag" Seesaw P-toy with Two Bears, 0132/24, L.E., 1988, $286. Right: Mr. Cinnamon Bear, 0151/25, L.E., 1904, 1984-1986, $190.

Teddy Bears

Steiff #	Description	80-81	81-82	82-83	83-84	84-85	85-86	86	87	88	89	90	Current
6992/30	Bear (Hand Puppet)	46	50	51	51	51	51	54	65			85	95
7492/05	Pitty Bear	6	7									15	17
7580/27	Toldi Bear SOS										82	82	89
8010/40	Riding Bear	185										355	367
8130/50	Riding Animal, Rocking Bear			285	295	295	295	310	375	600	600	385	416
8150/40	Riding Animal, Riding Bear Rocker		205	210	215	285	285	300				395	400
8155/50	Riding Animal, Bear on Wheels		285	290	295							565	575
8452/22	Broken Set Nimrod Bear, Caramel, LE					45						100	109
8453/22	Broken Set Nimrod Bear, White, LE					45		35				96	109
8455/22	Broken Set Nimrod Bear, Brass, LE					45						100	109

Margaret Woodbury Strong
Cream Bear, L.E., 1984-
1986. Left: 0157/60, $975.
Right: 0157/26, $161.

(Left) Bride, 0155/36, L.E. 2000 pieces, 1984 on, $241.
(Right) Groom, 0155/37, L.E. 2000 pieces, 1984 on, $241.

(Left) Ring Bearer, 0155/23, L.E. 2000 pieces, 1985-1988, $140.
(Right) Flower Bearer, 0155/22, L.E. 2000 pieces, 1985-1988, $140.

Margaret Woodbury Strong Cinnamon Bear Set, 0156/00, L.E., 1984-1986, $680. (Left) 0156/42, $224. (Right) 0156/32, $180.

Margaret Woodbury Strong Cinnamon Bear Set, 0156/00, L.E., 1984-1986, $680. (Left) 0156/18, $92. (Right) 0156/26, $115.

Left:
Margaret Woodbury Strong Chocolate Brown Set, 4 pieces, 0160/00, L.E. 2000 pieces, 1983-84.(Left) 0160/18, $100. (Right) 0160/26, $110.

Below:
(Left) 0160/32, $135. (Right) 0160/42, $150.

Margaret Strong Gold Bear, 0155/60, L.E., 1984 on, $549.

"The Birthplace of the Teddy," 0162/00, L.E. 16,000 pieces, 1984-1987, $300.

1909 Gold Teddy, 0165/51, L.E., 1984-1986, $487.

Teddy Baby, Brown, Replica 1930, 0175/32, L.E., 1984-1990, $98.

Teddy Baby, Brown, Replica 1930, 0175/42, L.E., 1984-1990, $330.

1938 Panda, Replica, 0178/35, L.E., 1984-1986, $320.

(Left)
White
Teddy
Bear,
0203/14,
L.E.,
1983-
1987, $81.
(Right)
Original
Teddy,
Caramel,
0202/18,
1983-
1990, $84.

(Left)
Hobby
Center
Toys store
special.
Panda,
0218/14,
L.E. 1000
pieces,
1988,
$350.
(Right)
Chocolate
Teddy
Bear,
0206/10,
L.E, 1984-
1986. $95.

Ophelia Bear, 0225/42, L.E., 1984-1990, $320. This bear was designed
by Michelle Clise. Because it was not designed by Steiff the tag and
button were not placed in the ear.

White Bear with Leather Paws, L.E.,, 1985-1987. (Left) 0158/41, $438. (Middle Front) 0158/25, $195. (Right) 0158/31, $325.

White Bear with Leather Paws, 0158/41, L.E., 1985-1987, $438.

Teddy "Jackie," 1953 Replica, 0190/25, L.E. 10,000 pieces, 1986-1987, $325.

Teddy Baby, 0178/32, Replica 1931, L.E., 1990, $225. In 1991 the Steiff tag number changed. For instance this bear for 1991 was tagged 408144.

Dicky Bear, 0172/32, L.E. 20,000 pieces, 1985-1988, $275.

Original Teddy, Grey, 0207/36, L.E., 1986-1990, $132.

Right:
Bear Dressed as Clown, White Tag, 0163/19, 1987, $220. This bear also came with a yellow tag and fetches less with collectors.

Below:
Circus Dolly Bear, L.E., 2000 pieces, white tag, 1987-1989. (Left) Yellow, 31cm, 0164/31, $204. (Center) Violet, 34cm, 0164/34, $204. (Right) Green, 32cm, 0164/32, $204.

Above:
Clifford Berryman Bear, 0255/35, L.E., 1987-1989,
$248.

Left:
(Left) Roly Poly Clown with Rattle, Replica 1909, 0116/28,
L.E., 1988-1990, $280. (Right) Roly Poly Bear with Rattle,
Replica 1908, 0115/18, L.E. 3000 pieces, 1988, $138.

Margaret Strong, Captain Strong, 0156/34, L.E., 1988-1989, $237.

Black Bear, 1907 Replica, 0173/40, L.E., 1988-1989, $535.

Muzzle Bear, White, 1908 Replica, 0174/60, L.E. 2650 pieces, 1989-1990, $550. Pictured in 60cm size this model also was produced in limited edi- tions; 35cm, L.E. 6000 pieces, 1990, $340 and 46cm, L.E. 5000 pieces, 1988-1990, $390.

Above:
Bear on 4 legs, univ. head movement, 0130/28, L.E. 4000 pieces, 1989-1990, $465.

Left:
Teddy Rose, 0171/25, L.E. 8000 pieces, 1990, $235.

White Original Bears with Paws, 0203/00, set of 5 pieces, set issued
1990 with white tags. Left to right: 0203/41cm, $240; 0203/18cm,
$104; 0203/11cm, $41; 0203/36cm, $180; and 0203/26cm, $115.

Teddy Bear Beige, 0201/14, L.E., 1983-1984, $81. Special costume from Festival of Steiff, Hobby Center Toys.

Bareback Bear Rider Set, 0145/00 (new number 650550), L.E. 5000 pieces, 1991, $435.

Steiff Wrist Watch Display with Teddy Baby & 13 Watches, 8530/00, 1991, $1325. (Note several watches in use by Teddy Bears.) Steiff is very innovative with providing clever accessories.

Suzanne Gibson Goldilocks and the Three (Steiff) Bears, 4004, $200. 8in Goldilocks, (Left to Right) 0173/18 mother, 0173/14 boy, 0173/22 father, L.E., 1985-1986. Reeves International Special.

Left: 1st Disney World Teddy Bear Convention, 0243/32, L.E., 500 pieces made (the tag erronously states 1000), 1988, $375 up. Note special metal Disney World logo.

Below: Suzanne Gibson Goldilocks and The Three (Steiff) Bears, 4003, $395. 16in Golidlocks, (left to right) 0173/25 boy, 0173/30 mother, 0173/32 father, L.E., 1984-1985. Reeves International Special.

Special Editions

Special Editions

Steiff #	Description	88	89	90	91	92	93	Current
00206	Teddy Donald, Walt Disney World, 6th Convention, LE						275	395
011863	Black Margaret Strong Bear with white bib, (referred to as Minnie Bear), Walt Disney World, 5th Convention, LE 1500					200		425 up
011979	Teddile, The Toy Store, LE 2000 announced, 1000 produced					125		*
011986	Light Grey Bear, Disneyland Convention, Anaheim, California, LE 1500					275		325 up
0152/25	Mr. Vanilla, Hobby Center Toys, LE 1000			**				335
0172/18	Dicky Mauve, Hobby Center Toys, LE 2000					**		275
0179/19	Dicky Rose, Hobby Center Toys, LE 2000				**			350
0218/14	Panda, Hobby Center Toys, mhr, LE 1000	**						350
0243/32	Gold Bear w/Red Ribbon, mhr, Walt Disney World, 1st Convention, LE 1000, only 500 produced.	95						400 up
0244/35	White Petsy Bear, Walt Disney World, 2nd Convention, LE 1000		115					325 up
0245/32	Grey Margaret Strong Bear, mhr, Walt Disney World, 3rd Convention, LE 1000			125				300 up
0246/32	Black Margaret Strong Bear with Mickey Mouse Mask (referred to as Mickey Bear), 32cm, Walt Disney World, 4th Convention, LE 1500				175			450 up
4003	Goldilocks 16" & Three Steiff Bears, Reeves International, (0173/25, Boy; 0173/30, Mother; 0173/32, Father), 1984, Offered at $200							695 up
4004	Goldilocks 8" & Three Steiff Bears, Reeves International, 0173/25, Boy; 0173/18, Mother; 0173/22 Father), 1985, Offered at $200							495 up
4005	Alice and Her Friends, (13cm Steiff Cat; 13cm Steiff Mouse; 20cm Steiff Rabbit with big pocket watch), LE 3000, 1986, Offered at $250							300 up
651847	Petsile, The Toy Store, LE 1500 announced, 950 produced						150	*

* Available from merchant at consumer price.

For photo of Hobby Center Toys and the Toy Store Special Editions, please refer to page 111.

(Left to Right) Crocodile Bandsman with Trumpet, 0124/19, $149; Cat Bandsman with Drum, 0122/19, $149; Bear Band Leader with Baton, 0120/19, $149; Dog Bandsman with Trombone, 0121/19, $149; Lion Bandsman with Tuba, 0123/19, $149. L.E., 1988-1989.

Circus Wagon Limited Edition Set, Left to Right: Circus Wagon with Two Bears, 0100/90, 1990, $495; Circus Wagon with Tiger, 0100/89, 1989, $605; Circus Wagon with Giraffe, 0100/88, 1988, $495.

Special Steiff Collectibles

Steiff #	Description	80-81	81-82	82-83	83-84	84-85	85-86	86	87	88	89	90	Current
0050/28	Dinosaur, 1959, LE 4000											200	220
0100/86	Elephant on Wheels w/Circus Calp., LE							300	300	300		1200	1320
0100/87	Circus Cage w/Lying Lion, LE								275			550	605
0100/88	Circus Wagon w/Giraffe, LE									325	450	495
0100/89	Circus Wagon w/Tiger, LE									350	550	605
0100/90	Circus Wagon w/Two Bears, LE											450	495
0118/00	Sleigh Set, mhr, LE 6000										275	275	320
0130/17	Unicorn, Lying, LE 2000				40	42						135	151
0130/27	Unicorn, Lying, LE 2000				55	57						175	196
0148/03	Teddy Bear Pin				9							15	20
0149/19	Fire Eater Dragon, mhr, LE 5000											125	138
0164/31	Circus Dolly Bear/Yellow, mhr, LE 2000 white tag							135	175	175	185	204
0164/32	Circus Dolly Bear/Green, mhr, LE 2000 white tag							135	175	175	185	204
0164/34	Circus Dolly Bear/Violet, mhr, LE 2000 white tag							135	175	175	185	204
6360/12	Teddy Shoulder Bag	10	11	12	12							22	33
6361/12	Teddy Coin Purse	10	11	12								22	33
6365/26	Teddy Shoulder Bag, Lg.	17	19	19	19							34	45
6370/22	Bear Music Box	49	54	54	54	54	54	54				97	99
6371/22	Cat Music Box	49										97	99
6376/18	Owl Music Box	44	48	49	49							88	95
6383/18	Ladybug Music Box	26	30									59	64
6400/15	Mosaic Ball, Sm., mhr	17	21	22								65	69
6400/20	Mosaic Ball, Med., mhr	28	32	32								110	115

Collectibles

Circus Wagon Cage with Lying Lion, 0100/87, 1987, $605; Elephant on Wheels with Circus Calliope, 0100/86, 1986, $1320. Limited Editions.

Special Steiff Collectibles

Steiff #	Description	80-81	81-82	82-83	83-84	84-85	85-86	86	87	88	89	90	Current
6450/15	Ball				21	21	21	22	27	42		45	49
6450/20	Ball				32	32	32	34	41	65		69	75
8470/17	Teeny Teddy Bag							60	77		80	86
8472/17	Teeny Bag Panda							60	55		60	65
8474/17	Teeny Bag Rabbit							60	55		60	65
8476/17	Teeny Bag Dog							60	55		60	65
8490/12	Teddy Minibag				12	12	12	15	22	22	23	24
8492/26	Teddy Bag				19	19	20	24	35		37	39
8494/03	Teddy Pin with Ribbon, mhr					20	19	19		22	30
8495/03	Teddy Pin, Beige, mhr				17	18	19	19		24	26
8496/03	Teddy Pin, Caramel, mhr				17	18	19	19		24	26
8497/03	Teddy Pin, White, mhr				17	18	19	19	19	24	26
8498/03	Teddy Pin, Chocolate, mhr				17	18	19	19	19	24	26
8500/03	Teddy Bear Pin				9	9	10	12	12	14	15
8501/02	Gold Plated Bar Pin w/Jointed Bear						15	18	27	22	29
8505/01	Gold Plated Teddy Earrings					20	21	27	46	46	46	50
8510/02	Gold Plated Teddy Necklace				15	15	16	20	32	32	30	32
8550/02	Reg Edition, History of Steiff									100	100	120
8601/06	Porcelain Tea Set, 7 pc.								18	15	20	29
8605/01	Wall Plate									9	9	10
8605/06	Mini Tea Set									15	15	16
8605/15	Deluxe Tea Set									57	57	62

Rabbits

Rabbits

Steiff #	Description	80-81	81-82	82-83	83-84	84-85	85-86	86	87	88	89	90	Current
0095/17	Begging Rabbit 7x Jntd 1911, LE 4000									145	145	145	165
0134/22	Niki Rabbit, mhr						58					155	185
0134/28	Niki Rabbit, mhr						70	75				195	211
0147/20	Rabbit, Begging								50	50		50	54
0155/00	Hoppy Rabbit Set, 3pc. 1984, LE					150	150	150				265	292
0338/34	Molly Rabbit		69	70	70	70						125	133
1350/10	Timmy Rabbit, Mini-Mohair										50	50	54
1350/12	Timmy Rabbit, Mini-Mohair										70	70	76
1500/09	Hoppy, Lying, Brown	14	17	18	18							32	35
1500/13	Hoppy, Beige					25	25	27	33			35	38
1501/09	Hoppy, Lying, Grey	14	17	18	18							32	35
1501/13	Hoppy, Grey					25	25	27	33			35	38
1502/10	Manni, Sitting, Brown	14	17									32	35
1502/15	Manni, Beige					25	25	27	33			35	38
1503/10	Manni, Sitting, Grey	14	17									45	49
1503/15	Manni, Grey					25	25	27	33			35	38
2882/25	Jr. Rabbit, Lying	38	38									75	83
2882/35	Jr. Rabbit, Lying	57	57									110	121
2910/12	Snuffy Rabbit, Brown	15	19	19								32	35
2910/18	Snuffy Rabbit, Brown	19	24	24								38	42
2911/12	Snuffy Rabbit, Grey	15	19	19								32	35
2911/18	Snuffy Rabbit, Grey	19	24	24								38	42
2931/16	Snuffy, Beige/White				29	29	29	30	38	55		55	59
2932/16	Snuffy, Caramel				29	29	29	30	38	55		55	59
2933/16	Snuffy, Dark Brown				29	29	29	30	38	55		55	59
2945/25	Rabbit	37	47	48								70	77
2947/35	Ossi, Standing	38	42									70	77
2950/32	Mummy Rabbit, Begging, Beige									120	125	125	135
2955/18	Winni, Grey, Sitting	30	33									60	66

Hoppy Rabbit Set,
0155/00, 3 pieces,
L.E., 1984, $292.

Rabbits

Steiff #	Description	80-81	81-82	82-83	83-84	84-85	85-86	86	87	88	89	90	Current
2955/32	Mummy Rabbit, Begging, Grey									120	125	125	135
2956/16	Hoppel Rabbit											37	39
2956/18	Winni, Brown, Sitting	30	33									60	66
2957/13	Hoppel, Grey	33	37	37	37							62	68
2957/22	Hoppel Rabbit											63	67
2958/13	Poppel, Beige	33	37	37	37							62	68
2958/25	Hoppel Rabbit											63	67
2960/22	Sonny, Grey	45	50	51	51	51	51	54	65			86	93
2961/22	Ronny, Beige	45	50	51	51	51	51	54	65			86	93
2962/16	Mummy, Grey	32	35	36	36							61	66
2962/25	Poppel Rabbit											63	67
2963/16	Pummy, Beige	32	35	36	36							60	66
2965/20	Rabbit, Sitting	29	35	35								46	51
2965/25	Rabbit, Sitting	38	50									70	77
2968/35	Snobby Rabbit				72	72	72	76	95			120	130
2970/23	B/W, Spotted	43	51	52	52	52						85	92
2970/30	B/W, Spotted	72	89	90	90							150	162
2972/40	Dormy Rabbit, Lying									165	175	110	119
2974/16	Dormili Rabbit							35	50	73	75	47	51
2975/25	Dormy Rabbit						67	71	86	120	125	75	81
2977/20	Dormili Rabbit							37	50	75		75	81
2978/35	Dormy Rabbit, Begging							115	160		165	165	178
2982/17	B/W Spottili, Running							55	75		80	80	86
2984/17	B/W Spottili, Sitting							53	73		75	75	81
2985/30	B/W Spotty, Sitting							100	140			140	151

Manni Rabbit Set, 3020/00 set number, 3 pieces, L.E., 1985-1987, $413. Left to Right: 3020/30cm, $195; 3020/10cm, $110; 3020/20, $153.

Rabbits

Steiff #	Description	80-81	81-82	82-83	83-84	84-85	85-86	86	87	88	89	90	Current
2992/17	Grey & White Spottili, Running								55	75	80	80	86
2994/17	Grey & White Spottili, Sitting								53	73	75	75	81
2995/30	Grey & White Spotty, Sitting								100	140	150	150	162
3020/00	Manni Rabbit Set, 3 pc., 1983, LE					175	175					375	413
3020/10	Manni Rabbit, mhr				35							95	110
3020/30	Manni Rabbit, mhr				75	75	75					175	195
3135/45	Ango	53	65	65								100	110
3141/43	Lulac, Brown, mhr	36	44									135	155
3142/43	Lulac, Grey, mhr	36										135	155
3155/16	Timmy, Brown	23	28	28	28							45	49
3156/16	Timmy, Grey	23	28	28	28							45	49
3480/40	Elbow Puppet-Rabbit, Grey	58	60	61	65	65	65	69	69			100	120
3480/41	Rabbit, White							69	69			115	124
3481/40	Elbow Puppet-Rabbit, Brown	58	60	61	65	65	65	69				110	132
5060/17	Pummy Rabbit										95	60	65
5060/21	Pummy Rabbit										130	83	89
5063/17	Pummy Rabbit										95	95	103
5063/21	Pummy Rabbit										130	130	140
5067/17	Pummy Rabbit										95	95	103
5067/21	Pummy Rabbit										130	130	140
5361/24	Cosy Manni			43	43	43						80	86
5362/24	Cosy Hoppy			43	43	43	43					80	86
5363/16	Cosy Snuffy, Beige			28	28	28	28	30	36			45	49
5364/16	Cosy Snuffy, Caramel			28	28	28	28		36			45	49
5502/13	Cosy Minni, Sitting, Beige/White									42	44	44	47
5503/13	Cosy Minni, Sitting, Brown/Cream									42	44	44	47
5504/13	Cosy Minni, Sitting, Grey/White									42	44	44	47
5505/13	Cosy Minni, Sitting, Black/White									42	44	44	47
5507/15	Manni, Begging, Brown/White									44	46	46	50
5508/15	Manni, Begging, Brown/Cream									44		44	48
5511/18	Cosy Snuffy, Crouching, Beige/White									60		60	65
5512/18	Cosy Snuffy, Crouching, Rust/Beige									60		60	65

Begging Rabbit, Replica 1911, 0095/17, L.E. 4000 pieces, 1988-1989, $165.

Rabbits

Steiff #	Description	80-81	81-82	82-83	83-84	84-85	85-86	86	87	88	89	90	Current
5513/16	Cosy Bunny, Aubergine											37	39
5514/16	Cosy Bunny, Blackberry											37	39
5525/25	Rabbit, Brown			50	50	50						92	99
5526/25	Ango, White		50	51	51	51						95	103
5605/18	Floppy Rabbit			36	36	36		38	48	69		69	75
5605/25	Floppy Rabbit			50	50	50			50			85	92
5658/16	Mini Floppy Rabbit										50	50	54
6060/24	Poppy Rabbit, Blond										80	80	86
6060/32	Poppy Rabbit, Blond										130	130	140
6062/24	Poppy Rabbit, Cinnamon										80	52	56
6062/32	Poppy Rabbit, Cinnamon										130	83	89
6067/24	Poppy Rabbit, Grey										80	80	86
6067/32	Poppy Rabbit, Grey										130	130	140
6235/30	Rabbit	40	40									70	77
6235/40	Rabbit	54	54									92	101
6280/40	Dangling Rabbit		52									90	97
6281/25	Lulac, Grey				43	43	46	57	80	83		55	59
6281/75	Lulac, Grey								200	300	300	195	211
6282/25	Lulac, Beige				43	43	46	57	80	83		55	59
6282/75	Lulac, Brown								200	300	300	300	324
6283/50	Lulac, Brown				72	72	72	76	92	130	135	86	93
6284/99	Lulac, Cream										575	575	621
6463/27	Rabbit (Hand Puppet)	30	33	33	33	33	33	35	42			55	62
6490/32	Happy Rabbit										105	105	113
6600/17	Rabbit (Hand Puppet), mhr	20										85	95
6993/30	Rabbit (Hand Puppet)	46	50	51	51	51	51	54	65			85	95
7010/45	Grey Jolly Rabbit Elbow Puppet									170		175	189
7136/04	Rabbits, Assmt	5	7	7	7	7						11	12
7146/06	Rabbits, Assmt	8	10	10	10	10	10	10	12			15	17
7156/08	Rabbits, Assmt	13	15	15	15	15	15	16	20			22	24

(Left) Lulac, Beige, 6282/25, 1984-1989, $59. (Right) Rabbit (Hand Puppet), 6463/27, 1980-1987, $62.

Above: (Left) Lulac Rabbit, Grey, 3142/43, 1980-1981, $155. (Right) Timmy Rabbit, Brown, 3155/16, 1980-1984, $49. *Photograph courtesy of Margarete Steiff GmbH and Reeves International.*

Left: Joggi Rabbit, 3145/55, 1981, $155. *Photograph courtesy of Margarete Steiff GmbH*

Cats

Cats

Steiff #	Description	80-81	81-82	82-83	83-84	84-85	85-86	86	87	88	89	90	Current
0104/10	Tabby Cat, 1928 Rep., LE 6000							75	75	120		130	143
0108/14	Drinking Cat, 1933, LE 4000											185	204
0122/19	Cat w/Drum, LE									125	125	135	149
0146/13	Cat, Crouching							50		50	50	50	54
0334/33	Molly Cat										175	175	189
1307/12	Kitty Cat, White, mhr											70	76
1314/12	Cat Kitty, Black, mhr											70	76
1493/13	Susi Cat, Grey			23	23	23	23	25	30	45		45	49
1493/14	Cat, Black			23	23	23						45	49
1495/10	Kitty Cat	14	16	17								39	43
1496/10	Black Tom Cat	22	24	25	25	25						52	57
2710/28	Cat Minka, Standing											92	98
2715/35	Cat Minka, Lying											84	89
2720/22	Cat, Grey	37	37									70	77
2725/22	Cat, Spotted	37	45									70	77
2726/17	Sissi Cat	35	38	39	39	39	39	41	50	75	75	47	52
2726/22	Sissi Cat	45	49	50	50	50	50	53	65	95		95	105
2728/17	Lizzy Cat	35	38	39	39	39	39	41	50	75	75	75	83

Cat, Lying, 2745/30, 1983-1985, $140.

57

Cats

Steiff #	Description	80-81	81-82	82-83	83-84	84-85	85-86	86	87	88	89	90	Current
2728/22	Lizzy Cat	45	49	50	50	50	50	53	65	95		95	105
2732/17	Tabby	35	38	39	39							75	83
2735/16	Sulla Cat, Cream					38	38	40				75	81
2735/26	Sulla Cat, Cream					58	58	61				105	113
2736/16	Sulla Cat, Grey					38	38	40	48	75		75	81
2736/26	Sulla Cat, Grey					58	58	61	75	105		105	113
2738/16	Dossy Cat, Black					38	38	40	48	75	75	75	81
2738/26	Dossy Cat, Black					58	58	61	75	105	105	105	113
2740/25	Siamese	57	63	64	64							120	132
2742/23	Cat								120	120		200	216
2745/30	Cat, Lying				75	75						130	140
2750/22	Ringel Cat, Lying		50	50	50							90	97
2752/26	Persian Cat, Grey			62	63	63	63					110	119
2752/35	Persian Cat, Grey			110	110	110						195	211
2753/26	Angora Cat, White			62	63	63	63					110	119
2754/25	Minou Cat, Lying, Cream							70	85	120	120	120	130
2754/40	Minou Cat, Lying, Cream							100	125	175	175	120	130
2755/25	Minou Cat, Lying, Grey							70	85	120		120	130
2755/40	Minou Cat, Lying, Grey							100	125	175		175	189
2756/25	Minou Cat, Lying, Black							70	85	120	120	120	130
2756/40	Minou Cat, Lying, Black							100	125	175		175	189
2757/25	Minou Cat, Striped								92	120	120	120	130
2757/40	Minou Cat, Striped								130	175	175	175	189
2758/40	Cat									175	175	175	189
2926/16	Snuffy Cat				32	32	32					55	59
2927/16	Snuffy Cat				32	32	32					55	59
2928/16	Snuffy Cat								50	65	65	42	45
3483/40	Elbow Puppet-Cat	70	76									135	162
3520/12	Snuffy Cat, Beige	17	21	22								36	40
3520/17	Snuffy Cat, Beige	22	28									40	44
3521/12	Snuffy Cat, Grey	17	21	22								36	40
3521/17	Snuffy Cat, Grey	22	28	29								40	44

7

Mizzi Cat, Grey, 2720/22, 1980-1982, $77.00. *Photograph courtesy of Margarete Steiff GmbH*

9

Mizzi Cat, Spotted, 2725/22, 1980-1982, $77. *Photograph courtesy Margarete Steiff GmbH.*

Cats

Steiff #	Description	80-81	81-82	82-83	83-84	84-85	85-86	86	87	88	89	90	Current
5440/16	Cosy Sulla, Cream						40	43	52	52		52	56
5440/22	Cosy Sulla, Cream						50	53	65			65	70
5442/16	Cosy Milla, Blonde						40	43	52			52	56
5442/22	Cosy Milla, Blonde						50	53	65	65		65	70
5520/25	Cat, Grey			50	50	50	50					90	97
5620/18	Floppy Cat				36	36	36	38	48	70		60	65
5620/25	Floppy Cat				50	50	50	53	65	100		100	107
5665/16	Mini Floppy Cat										50	50	54
5717/20	Kiddi Cat										75	75	81
5720/20	Cat	39	43									69	76
5720/30	Cat	57	62									100	110
5780/22	Drolly Cat											52	55
6080/32	Poppy Cat									135		135	146
6225/28	Possy Cat										115	115	125
6275/27	Toldi Cat									90		90	97
6285/60	Dangling Tomcat	105										185	204
6290/32	Dangling Cat "Burri"							60	72	110		110	119
6466/27	Cat (Hand Puppet)	30	33	33	33							55	62
6494/32	Happy Cat										115	115	124
6660/17	Cat, Grey (Hand Puppet), mhr	20										85	95
6998/30	Cat	46	50									85	95
7494/05	Pitty Cat	6	7									9	10

(Left) Drink Cat, 0108/14, Replica 1933, L.E. 4000 pieces, 1990, $204. (Right) Kitty Cat, 1307/12, 1990, $76.

Dogs

Steiff #	Description	80-81	81-82	82-83	83-84	84-85	85-86	86	87	88	89	90	Current
0101/14	Bully Dog, 1927 Rep., LE 6000							75	75	120		145	160
0118/25	Boxer, Lying, mhr, LE 2000				55	57	57	57	57			85	151
0121/19	Dog w/Trombone, LE									125	125	135	149
0332/33	Molly Dog										175	175	189
0337/50	Schnauzer	138	170									270	297
0338/35	Molly Chow	63	76									115	127
0338/60	Molly Chow	145	175									230	253
0340/35	Molly Husky	72	89									115	127
0340/60	Molly Husky	145	175									230	253
0342/40	S-Molly St. Bernard					80	80					130	140
0342/60	S-Molly St. Bernard					150	150					245	265
0342/80	S-Molly St. Bernard					275	275	295				450	486
0342/98	S-Molly St. Bernard					400	400	425				660	713
0342/99	Super Molly Dog		680	700	700							1050	1134
0343/50	Molly Bello Dog								185		185	185	200
0350/45	Molly Dog		95	98	98	98						180	194
0350/65	Molly Dog		157	160	160							295	319
0460/45	Molly Husky										195	125	135
0460/60	Molly Husky										330	330	356
1306/12	Waldi Hound, Tan, mhr											70	76
1313/12	Hound Waldi, Brown, mhr											70	76
1526/11	Dog	13	15									34	37
1528/11	Fox Terrier	15	18	19	19	27	27					36	40
1530/12	Schnauzer	17	19									40	44
1532/12	Poodle, Black	18	20	21	21	21						40	44
1533/12	Poodle, White	18	20	21	21	21						40	44
2882/35	Jr. Fox Terrier			81	89	89	89	95				165	178
2883/30	Jr. Schnauzer, Sitting	67										120	132
2883/35	Jr. Charly Dog			81	81	81	81	86				140	151
2884/26	Jr. Cockie		75	75	75							125	135
2884/30	Jr. Schnauzer, Lying	67										120	132
2885/28	Dog, Sitting	59	70									110	121
2886/28	Dog, Lying	59	70									110	121
2887/26	Swiss Mtn Dog			75	75							140	151
2888/35	St. Bernard	90	110	115	115							170	187
2890/22	Jr. Pekinese			53	53	53	53					95	103
2893/30	Jr. Scotch Terrier			74	74	74						135	146
2923/16	Snuffy Dog			32	32	32		34	42	62		62	67
3492/45	Mimic Dog				75	75	75	79	95			120	130
4010/12	Mopsy Dog, mhr	17	20									75	79
4026/21	Spaniel "Cockie", Sitting											74	80
4028/32	Spaniel "Cockie", Lying											88	95
4030/14	Pekinese		40	41	41	43	43					75	81
4035/38	Cocker Spaniel					80	80	85	110	150		150	162
4040/99	St. Bernard Dog	450	615	610	665							1065	1200
4045/35	Boxer				80	80	80	85	105	175	175	175	189
4045/50	Boxer, Lying			130	130	130	130	138	165	250	250	105	113
4048/40	German Shepherd				80	80	80					135	146
4048/50	German Shepherd			130	130	130	130	138	165	250		250	270
4050/80	Shepherd, Standing	665	775	796	796							1200	1320
4052/80	Shepherd, Lying	565	625	639	639							1075	1182
4053/20	German Shepherd Puppy				33	33	33					55	59
4053/23	Shepherd, Puppy	66	74	75	75	75	75					125	138
4055/65	Husky	580	650									995	1095
4060/80	Setter, Standing	520	600									1000	1100
4061/80	Setter, Sitting	520	600	602	602							1100	1210
4065/65	Chow	545	600	602	602	585						1000	1100
4070/55	Schnauzer	245	275	285	285							490	539
4075/60	Boxer	500	575	575	745	745						1110	1221
4080/50	Terrier	255	285	285	285	285						490	539
4085/28	Terrier	72	79									135	149
4090/40	Collie				80	80	80	85	110			160	173
4121/30	Pomeranian, White	72	80	82	82							135	149

Dogs

Steiff #	Description	80-81	81-82	82-83	83-84	84-85	85-86	86	87	88	89	90	Current
4122/30	Pomeranian, Rust	72	80									135	149
4130/20	"Mobby" Bobtail Dog, Sitting									80	80	80	86
4132/24	"Mobby" Bobtail Dog, Standing									125	125	125	135
4140/30	Fox Terrier "Treff"									145	145	92	98
4142/12	Dachshund	24	26	27	27	30	30	32				45	50
4150/25	Raudi Dachshund, Sand/Grey							75	90	135		135	146
4150/40	Raudi Dachshund, Sand/Grey							100	125	190		190	205
4151/25	Raudi Dachshund, Grey/Brown							75	90	135		135	146
4151/40	Raudi Dachshund, Grey/Brown							100	125	190		190	205
4153/25	Dog Raudi											98	104
4156/26	Poodle, Brown	55	60									105	116
4157/26	Poodle, Black	55	60									105	116
4157/50	Poodle, Standing	255	285	285	285							495	545
4158/50	Poodle, Upright	275	300									540	594
4160/24	Welfo Puppy, Standing							95	125	125		125	135
4160/35	Poodle, Black	67	74									120	132
4161/35	Poodle, White	67	74									120	132
4162/22	Welfo Puppy, Lying							100	135			140	151
4162/35	Poodle, Apricot	67	74									120	132
4165/45	Wolfi Dog, Lying							225	300			320	346
4167/40	Shepherd Dog "Arco", Sitting											135	143
4168/45	Shepherd Dog Arco, Lying											170	180
4180/45	Afgan Dog, Standing							235	315			325	351
4182/40	Afgan Dog, Sitting							175	230			245	260
4184/35	Blacky S. Terrier									160	160	173
4185/35	Whity W.H. Terrier									160	160	173
4192/25	Yorkshire Terrier, Sitting							125	165	165		165	178
4215/21	Fox Terrier	48	52									85	94
4215/30	Fox Terrier	73										135	149
5368/33	Cosy Dog								95			95	103
5445/20	Cosy Poodle "Tobby", Stndg, Apricot							50	60	90		90	97
5445/28	Cosy Poodle "Tobby", Stndg, Apricot							70	87	135		135	146
5447/20	Cosy Poodle Tobby, Stndg, Black							50	60	90		90	97
5447/28	Cosy Poodle "Tobby", Stndg, Black							70	87	135		135	146
5452/28	Cosy Poodle "Nobby", Lying, Grey							75	90	135		135	146
5457/20	Cosy Dog "Bello" Standing, Grey							50	60	90		90	97
5457/27	Cosy Bello-Dog				63	63						100	108

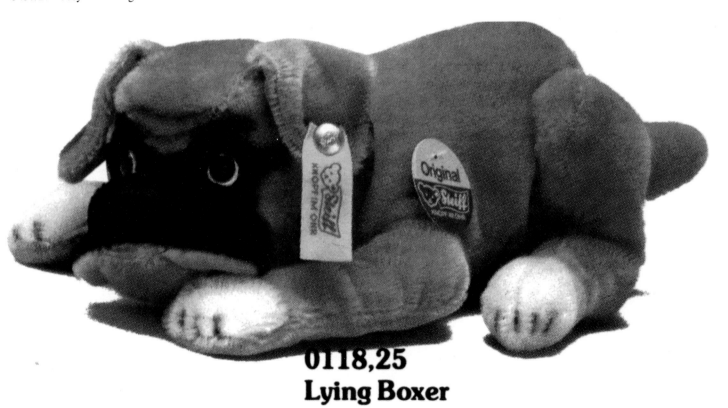

0118,25
Lying Boxer

Boxer, Lying, 0118/25, L.E. 2000 pieces, 1983-1987, $94. *Photograph courtesy Margarete Steiff GmbH and Reeves International.*

Dogs

Steiff #	Description	80-81	81-82	82-83	83-84	84-85	85-86	86	87	88	89	90	Current
5460/35	Cosy Daschund			81	81	81	81					145	157
5463/50	Cosy Basset Dog				125	125	135	165		225		225	243
5465/16	Cosy Lumpi Schnauzer					34	36	44	70			70	76
5465/27	Cosy Lumpi Schnauzer					55	58	71	120			120	130
5466/16	Cosy Lumpi Schnauzer, Lying					36	38	46	75			75	81
5530/25	Cuddly Dog			50	50							90	97
5610/18	Floppy Dog				36	36	38	38	48	70		70	76
5610/25	Floppy Dog				50							85	92
5662/16	Mini Floppy Dog										53	53	57
5712/20	Kiddi Dog										75	75	81
5717/20	Terrier	41	44									75	83
5717/30	Terrier	59	65									100	110
5820/22	Dog	43	48									79	87
6276/27	Toldi Dog									80		80	86
6284/60	Dangling Dog	105	115									185	204
6287/70	Dangling Dog											220	233
6291/32	Dangling Dog "Lumpi"							60	72	110		110	119
6464/27	Dog (Hand Puppet)	30	32									55	62
6640/17	Fox Terrier (Hand Puppet), mhr	20										85	95
6994/30	Dog (Hand Puppet)	46	50									85	95
7497/05	Pitty Dog	6	7									9	10
7690/20	Shepard	31	34									60	69

Hector, 4075/60, Studio, 1980-1985, $1221. *Photograph courtesy Margarete Steiff GmbH.*

Farmyard Animals

Farmyard Animals

Steiff #	Description	80-81	81-82	82-83	83-84	84-85	85-86	86	87	88	89	90	Current
0081/14	Felt Duck, 1892 Rep., LE 4000									125	125	125	138
0091/14	Pig, Univ Head Movement, 1909, LE 4000										155	155	171
0126/20	Donkey Mechanical 1909 Rep, LE									185	185	185	204
0145/12	Lamb								30	30		30	32
0335/55	Molly Donkey		95	98	98	98	98	105	125	175		180	194
0335/80	Molly Donkey	185	250									370	407
0336/55	Molly Pony		95	98								198	214
0360/45	Molly Pig		95	98	98	98	98	105	125	175		180	194
0361/90	Super Molly Pig			275	275	275	295	375		525	525	310	341
0363/40	Molly Zicky Goat											115	124
0363/50	Molly Zicky Goat											150	162
0365/40	Molly Pony, Brown									125	125	77	83
0365/50	Molly Pony								175	235		235	254
0365/99	Super Molly Cow			400	400	400						700	770
0366/99	Super Molly Pony			400	400	400	425					700	770
0367/40	Molly Pony, Black									125		125	135
0367/99	Super Molly Donkey			400	400	400	425	425				700	770
0370/40	Molly Lamb		74	76	76	76						140	151
0440/99	Goat										3550	3000	3300
0445/60	Little Goat										1000	575	633

Pig, Universal Head Movement, 0091/14, Replica 1909, L.E. 4000 pieces, 1989-1990, $171.

Molly Lamby, 0370/40, 1981-1985, $151.

Farmyard Animals

Steiff #	Description	80-81	81-82	82-83	83-84	84-85	85-86	86	87	88	89	90	Current
0446/60	Little Goat										1000	575	633
0450/99	Donkey										3975	3995	4395
0453/75	Little Donkey										2750	2000	2200
1505/10	Piggy Pig		22	23	23	23	23	25	30	45	45	30	33
1510/14	Donkey	17	19	21	23	29	29					45	49
1516/14	Pony	17	20	21	23	17	17	29				34	37
1518/11	Lamb	13	16	17	17	17	17	18	22			40	44
1520/11	Sheep, B/W	13	16	17	17	17	17	18	22			40	44
1522/14	Horse								38	58	58	37	40
1524/12	Cow								38	58	58	58	62
1525/08	Pig								34	50	50	50	54
1526/12	Brown Baby Goat								36	50	55	55	59
1527/12	White Baby Lamb								36	50	55	55	59
1834/40	Lamb	66										120	132
2918/18	Snuffy Pig								50	66	66	66	71
3205/15	Tulla Duck	23	27	28	28	28	28	30	36			43	47
3210/16	Willa Duck, Green									46	48	48	52
3210/22	Willa Duck, Green									60		60	65
3211/16	Pilla Duck, Blue									46		50	54
3211/22	Pilla Duck, Blue									60		60	65
3215/16	Tulla Duck, Red									46		50	54
3215/22	Tulla Duck, Red									60		60	65
3230/11	Duck Daggi										35	35	38
3232/11	Duck Daggi										35	35	38

Farmyard Animals

Steiff #	Description	80-81	81-82	82-83	83-84	84-85	85-86	86	87	88	89	90	Current
3240/16	Duck Waggi											35	37
3240/20	Duck Waggi											48	51
3242/08	Piccy Duck	10		11								25	38
3242/11	Piccy Duck	14	16	16								32	35
3243/16	Duck Waggi											35	37
3243/20	Duck Waggi											48	51
3450/22	Locky Lamb	36	40									72	79
3455/17	Zicky Goat			38	38	38						70	76
3455/23	Zicky Goat			60	60							100	108
3460/20	Rocky Wild Goat			41	43	43						80	86
3460/25	Lamb Lamby									77		77	83
3460/30	Lamb Lamby									95		95	103
3462/22	Lamb Lamby									65		43	46
3464/22	Lamb Lamby, Brown									65		43	46
3605/20	Donkey	29	36	37								56	62
3605/27	Donkey	39	47									75	83
3710/60	Pony on Wheels	225										675	695
3750/18	Pony, Brown, mhr	24	29									120	125
3760/25	Horse, Brown	57	63	64	65	65	65					110	119
3785/25	Horse, Beige	53	58	59	59							100	110
3790/18	Calf	34	38	38								65	72
3792/25	Cow	57	63	64	64							110	121
3795/27	Calf, Lying			66	72	72	72	76	93			115	124
3810/17	Pig	34	38	38	38	38	38	40	48	70	70	45	55
5360/25	Cosy Pony			45	46	46	46					85	92
5360/40	Pony	76	83	85	85	85						135	149
5376/11	Preppy Duck, Boy						20	21	28	40		40	43
5376/12	Preppy Duck, Girl						20	21	28	40		40	43
5377/12	Cosy Piccy Duck			17	18	18	18					32	35
5378/17	Cosy Daggi Duck			21	22	22	22	23				39	42
5414/18	Cosy Piggy Pig						30	32	39	63	63	40	43

(Left) Zicky Goat, 3455/17, 1982-1985, $75. (Right) Donkey, 0126/20, Replica 1909, L.E., 1988-1990, $204.

Farmyard Animals

Steiff #	Description	80-81	81-82	82-83	83-84	84-85	85-86	86	87	88	89	90	Current
5415/28	Cosy Pig			49	52	52	52	55	66	100	95	61	66
5472/20	Cosy Grissy Donkey							44	53	80	80	80	86
5472/28	Cosy Grissy Donkey					66	66	70	87	87		87	94
5473/25	Cosy Lamby							52	71	110		110	119
5473/40	Cosy Lamby							72	115	175		175	189
5474/21	Cosy Lamb						39	41	50	70		70	76
5474/27	Cosy Lamb						60	65	78	115		115	124
5475/20	Cosy Horse "Ferdy", Brown							44	53	80	80	50	54
5475/28	Cosy Horse "Ferdy"						59	62	75	125	125	125	135
5476/20	Cosy Horse "Yello", Beige							44	53	80		80	86
5477/25	Cosy Flora Cow						59	62	75	125		125	135
5480/22	Cosy Zicky Goat							70	100			110	119
5491/18	Gocki Rooster								58	85	85	85	92
5495/18	Gacki Hen								58	85	85	85	92
5498/10	Cosy Bibi Chick								19	27		30	32
5625/18	Floppy Lamb				36	36	36	38	48	65		70	76
5625/25	Floppy Lamb				50	50	50	53	65	95		95	103
5668/16	Mini Floppy Lamb										50	50	54
5672/16	Mini Floppy Donkey										53	53	57
5675/16	Mini Floppy Pig										50	50	54
5725/20	Floppy Lamb			41								75	81
5725/30	Floppy Lamb			59								110	119
6202/14	Friedericke, Yellow Goose									47	49	31	33

Super Molly Cow, 0365/99, 1983-1986, $770. (Smaller animal) Calf, Lying, 3795/27, 1982-1987, $124.

Farmyard Animals

Steiff #	Description	80-81	81-82	82-83	83-84	84-85	85-86	86	87	88	89	90	Current
6203/26	Friedericke Ylw Goose, Drsd Grl									80	85	85	92
6205/14	Frederic, White Gander									47	49	31	33
6206/26	Frederic, White Gander									80	85	85	92
6210/20	Cuddly Goose, Yellow										65	65	70
6210/32	Cuddly Goose, Yellow										100	100	108
6212/20	Cuddly Goose, Brown										65	65	70
6212/32	Cuddly Goose, Brown										100	100	108
6212/50	Cuddly Goose, Brown										200	200	216
6422/24	Donkey Pull Toy			62								115	120
6996/30	Donkey (Hand Puppet)	46										85	95
7212/08	Duckling	9	10									14	15
7240/08	Rooster	7	8	8								11	12
7245/08	Rooster	9	11	11	11							16	18
7250/08	Hen	7	8	8								11	12
7255/08	Hen	9	11	11	11	11						16	18
7260/04	Chick	4	5	6	6							8	9
7260/06	Chick	5	7	7	7	7						10	11
7260/08	Chick	9	11	11	11							16	18
7496/05	Pitty Lamb	6	7									9	10
8020/45	Rocking Duck	150											
8135/50	Riding Animal, Rocking Pony			285	295	295	295	310	375	600	600	385	416
8175/60	Riding Animal, Pony on Wheels		295	300	300							570	585
8195/45	Riding Animal, Rocking Duck		175	180	175	175	175					330	350

Riding Animal, Rocking Pony, 8135/50, 1982-1989, $416.

67

Woodland Animals

Woodland Animals

Steiff #	Description	80-81	81-82	82-83	83-84	84-85	85-86	86	87	88	89	90	Current
0055/00	Eric Bat Set, 2 pc., 1960, LE 4000											200	220
0093/12	Fox, 1910, LE 4000										150	150	165
0345/25	Molly Woodchuck		43	43	43	43						80	86
0346/30	Molly Groundhog	48	57	58	58	58	58	61	75	115		120	132
0347/55	Fox		148	150	150	150	150	160	195			280	302
0348/22	Molly Raccoon	42	52	53								110	121
1308/12	Mouse Fiep, Grey, mhr											60	65
1310/12	Mouse Fiep, White, mhr											60	65
1311/12	Fox Fuzzy, mhr											70	76
1312/12	Possy Squirrel, mhr											70	76
1464/12	Fox Woodland Animal							25	34	50		50	54
1465/10	Fox	19	21	22	22	24	24	26	32			45	50
1466/12	Squirrel Woodland Animal							25	36	50	50	32	35
1467/10	Squirrel	17	19	20	20	20	20					39	43
1470/12	Paddy Beaver		20	21	21	21	21	22	27	40	40	40	43
1476/12	Marmot Woodland Animal							25	34	50	50	50	54
1480/12	Ermine Woodland Animal							25	34			50	54
1540/20	Xorry Fox, Lying							40	48	70	70	46	50
1542/35	Red Fox, Sleeping	67	75	76	76	76	76	80	96	120	120	74	85

Screech Owl, 2593/28, 1981-1988, $211.

Frog, Dangling,
2380/32, 1980-1985, $60.

Woodland Animals

Steiff #	Description	80-81	81-82	82-83	83-84	84-85	85-86	86	87	88	89	90	Current
1543/35	Raccoon, Sleeping	67	67									175	188
1544/35	Fox, Sleeping, Beige	70	78	79	79							175	195
1548/25	Fuzzy Fox										115	78	84
1550/12	Owl Woodland Animal							25	30	50	50	31	33
1670/06	Hedgehog, Lying, mhr	4	5	5	6	6	6	7	8	14	14	14	15
1670/10	Hedgehog, Lying, mhr	9	10	13	14	16	16					44	48
1670/17	Hedgehog, Lying, mhr	17	21	23	25	28	28					75	83
1675/12	Joggi Hedgehog						18	19	23	40	40	25	27
1675/18	Joggi Hedgehog						24	25	30	50	50	50	54
1675/35	Hedgehog Joggi											93	100
1675/45	Super Joggi Hedgehog							60	145	220		220	238
1675/70	Super Joggi Hedgehog							295	360	500		500	540
1677/14	Joggi Hedgehog, Begging						24	25	30	50	50	32	35
1677/20	Hedgehog Joggi											46	50
1677/50	Hedgehog									350		350	378
1680/12	Hedgehog, Begging, mhr	16	20	21	22	22	22					70	77
1820/14	Fawn	24	26	27	27							58	64
1830/40	Deer, Standing	85	95	98								155	171
1831/20	Fawn, Lying									75	75	48	52
1831/38	Fawn, Lying	55	63	64	64	64	64	68	82	100	100	100	109
1835/22	Fawn, Standing									100	100	100	107
1837/30	Doe, Lying									120	120	120	130
1838/30	Roebuck, Standing									145	145	145	157
1840/26	Diggy Badger							60	72	110		115	124

Woodland Animals

Steiff #	Description	80-81	81-82	82-83	83-84	84-85	85-86	86	87	88	89	90	Current
1840/36	Diggy Badger							80	100	150		165	178
2015/24	Squirrel									135	135	86	93
2025/18	Chipmunk Chippy										90	60	65
2030/20	Squirrel	31	37	38						75		58	64
2032/25	Possy Squirrel			41	41	41	41	44				75	81
2040/12	Perri Squirrel, mhr	18	22	23	23							85	94
2040/17	Perri Squirrel, mhr	22										110	121
2042/24	Marmot Piff, Grey/Brown											63	68
2050/25	Raggy Racoon, Standing							95	125	125		81	87
2055/35	Raggy Racoon, Sitting							145	195	195		120	130
2060/20	Raggy Ringel Racoon							65	90	90		57	62
2070/25	Piff Marmot, Standing							85	110	110		110	119
2080/35	Skunk										160	105	113
2121/18	Beaver	29										55	61
2125/20	Nagy Beaver		34	35	35	35	35	37	37			65	70
2150/12	Goldy Hamster						24	25	30	50		50	54
2150/16	Goldy Hamster						29	31	38	62		65	70
2150/50	Super Goldy Hamster						295	310	310	310		310	335
2155/12	Hamster	17	20	21	21	21						34	37
2155/17	Hamster	22	27	27	27	27						42	46
2170/10	Mouse, White	11	13	14	14	14	14	15	18	30	30	30	33
2171/10	Mouse, Grey	11	13	14	14	14	14	15	18	30	30	30	33
2180/12	Mole/Shovel, mhr	11	14	18	19	19	19	20	24	40		45	55
2180/15	Maxi Mole	22	29	30	30	30	30					45	50
2205/12	Woodchuck	24	26	27	27	27	27					49	54

Opposite Page: Super Goldy Hamster, 2150/50, 1985-1988, $335.

Right: Felt Duck, 0081/14, Replica 1892, L.E. 4000 pieces, 1988-1990, $138.

Woodland Animals

Steiff #	Description	80-81	81-82	82-83	83-84	84-85	85-86	86	87	88	89	90	Current
2252/10	Guinea Pig	19	21	22	22	22	22	23	28	40		42	46
2254/15	Guinea Pig					29	29	31				48	52
2255/15	Guinea Pig, Mama	24	30									49	54
2256/15	Guinea Pig, Papa	24	30	31	31							48	53
2270/22	Mouse Pieps, Grey											66	71
2275/22	Mouse Pieps, White											66	71
2370/08	Frog, Sitting	17	20	21	21	24	24	26	32			39	41
2380/32	Frog, Dangling	29	32	32	32	32						57	60
2455/14	Turtle	19	23	24	24	24						85	89
2455/22	Turtle	36										135	142
2460/30	Ladybug/Wheels, mhr	145										445	450
2580/14	Raven Hucky											45	49
2590/50	Owl		295									475	513
2591/22	Owlet		50	50	50	50	50	53	65	90	90	90	97
2592/25	Baby Owl "Wiggy"											59	64
2593/28	Screech Owl		97	99	99	99	99	105	125	190		195	211
2603/28	Woodpecker, Spotted	82	82									158	165
2604/28	Woodpecker, Green	82	82									158	165
2622/18	Wittie Eagle Owl								55	75	75	75	81
2622/24	Wittie Eagle Owl								89	120		120	130
2622/40	Pheasant	260	295	295	295							495	500
2623/40	Golden Pheasant	275	300	315	315							550	600
2625/15	Owl	26	30	31	31	31	31	33	40			58	63
2625/25	Owl	41	50	50	50							80	88

Fox, 0093/12, Replica 1910, L.E. 4000 pieces, 1989-1990, $165.

Woodland Animals

Steiff #	Description	80-81	81-82	82-83	83-84	84-85	85-86	86	87	88	89	90	Current
2881/35	Fox, Crouching	70	85									140	154
2892/28	Jr. Fuzzy Fox		79	80	80							150	162
2916/16	Snuffy Fox							50	67	67		67	72
3476/40	Elbow Puppet-Skunk	80	87	88								150	180
3477/50	Elbow Puppet-Raccoon	80	87	88								150	180
3515/14	Snuffy Fox	19	24									38	42
3515/18	Snuffy Fox	25	32									50	55
4900/22	Fox	22										42	46
5250/17	Fox Pummy									100		66	71
5250/21	Fox Pummy									135		88	93
5382/43	Cosy Froggy		70									135	146
5384/16	Cosy Froggy Frog							44	53	80	80	52	56
5384/20	Cosy Froggy Frog					44		47	57	57		57	62
5384/28	Cosy Froggy Frog					75		80	96	96		96	104
5384/50	Super Cosy Froggy Frog							325	395	395		445	481
5390/30	Cosy Mouse, Blue		42									80	86
5391/30	Cosy Mouse, Violet		42									80	84
5392/15	Cosy Mouse, Olive		22										
5392/30	Cosy Mouse, Green		42	43	43	43	43					80	86
5393/15	Cosy Mouse, White		22	23	23	23	23					40	43
5393/45	Cosy Fiep Mouse, White							145	190			190	205
5394/15	Cosy Mouse, Grey		22	23	23							40	43
5394/45	Cosy Fiep Mouse, Grey								145	190		190	205
5396/17	Cosy Nagy Beaver							31	40	60	60	60	65

(Left) Mole/Shovel, 2180/12, 1980-1988, $55. (Middle) Fox Fuzzy, 1311/12, 1990, $76. (Right) Mouse, Fiep, White, 1310/12, 1990, $65.

Woodland Animals

Steiff #	Description	80-81	81-82	82-83	83-84	84-85	85-86	86	87	88	89	90	Current
5396/22	Cosy Nagy Beaver							46	65	95		95	103
5397/15	Cosy Hedgehog		20	21	21	21	21					39	42
5397/25	Cosy Joggi Hedgehog		30	30	30	30						55	59
5432/20	Snail "Nelly", Purple							55				55	59
5434/20	Snail Nelly, Brown							55				55	59
5558/10	Mini Cosy Hedgehog							15	18	28	28	28	30
5565/10	Blue Bird								19	30		32	35
5567/10	Brown Bird								19	30		32	35
5678/16	Mini Floppy Fox										53	53	57
5722/20	Kiddi Mouse										75	75	81
5725/20	Kiddi Hedgehog										75	75	81
5728/20	Kiddi Fox										75	75	81
5790/22	Drolly Fox											52	55
6020/32	Poppy Raccoon										135	135	146
6215/30	Fox	40										72	79
6240/28	Possy Fox									120	78		84
6245/28	Possy Hedgehog									115	115		124
6273/27	Toldi Hedgehog									80	80	80	86
6274/27	Toldi Frog									80		80	86
6292/32	Dangling Frog "Cappy"							60	72	110		110	119
6294/32	Dangling Mouse "Pieps"							60	72			110	119
6462/27	Frog (Hand Puppet)	26	28									50	56
6470/27	Owl (Hand Puppet)	30	33									55	62
6472/27	Fox (Hand Puppet)	33	36									62	69

Eric Bat Set, Replica 1960, 0055/00, L.E. 4000, 1990, $220.

Woodland Animals

Steiff #	Description	80-81	81-82	82-83	83-84	84-85	85-86	86	87	88	89	90	Current
6496/32	Happy Hedgehog										95	95	103
6497/32	Happy Fox										115	115	124
6995/30	Owl (Hand Puppet)	50	55									85	95
7170/06	Guniea Pig	9	9									15	17
7173/06	Hampster	8	8									12	13
7180/05	Frog	7	8	8	8							14	15
7180/07	Frog	8	10	10	10							16	18
7354/04	Mouse, White	5	7	7	7							9	10
7355/04	Mouse, Grey	5	7	7	7							9	10
7370/03	Lady Bug	5	6	7								9	10
7370/04	Lady Bug	4	5	5	6							7	8
7370/06	Lady Bug	5	7	7	8							9	10
7480/06	Owl	7	9	9	9							12	13
7480/09	Owl	9	11	11	11							16	18
7493/05	Pitty Fox	6	7									9	10
7502/05	Pitty Squirrel	6	7									9	10
7503/05	Pitty Mice	8	9									14	15
7860/20	Bambi Fawn					34	34	36				75	95
8190/30	Riding Animal, Ladybug/Wheels		185	190	195	195	195	205	250	375		350	375

Spider Set, 0054/00 (also 401800), Set of 2, Museum Edition, 1991, $335.

Characters

(Left) Man Mecki Character, 7627/28, 1980-1990, $155.
(Middle) Boy Mecki Character, 7627/12, 1980-1990, $49.
(Right) Man Mecki Character, 7627/17, 1980-1990, $99.

(Left) Woman Mecki Character, 7628/28, 1980-1990, $155.
(Middle) Woman Mecki Character, 7628/17, 1980-1990, $99.
(Right) Girl Mecki Character, 7628/12, 1980-1990, $49.

Steiff #	Description	80-81	81-82	82-83	83-84	84-85	85-86	86	87	88	89	90	Current
0116/28	Roly Poly Clown w/Rattle 1909, mhr, LE									260	260	260	280
0155/22E	Santa's Elf, LE									100	100	125	138
0156/34	M. Strong Captain Strong, LE									200	200	215	237
0156/36	M. Strong Victorian Lady, LE								150	150	150	195	215
0156/37	M. Strong Victorian Man, LE								150	150	150	195	215
0156/38	Vic. Santa Bxd, 1200 pc., 1987								150	200	200	200	210
1523/20	Shepherd and His Flock	69	80									320	352
7627/12	Boy Mecki Character	13	16	17	18	20	20	21	27	45	45	45	49
7627/17	Man Mecki Character	32	39	39	41	50	50	53	65	95	95	95	99
7627/28	Man Mecki Character	50	60	61	65	70	70	75	90	145	145	145	155
7627/50	Mecki, Man			180	195	195	195					340	355
7628/12	Girl Mecki Character	13	16	17	18	20	20	21	27	45	45	45	49
7628/17	Woman Mecki Character	32	39	39	41	50	50	53	65	95	95	95	99
7628/28	Woman Mecki Character	50	60	61	65	70	70	75	90	145	145	145	155
7628/50	Mecki, Woman			180	195	195	195					340	355
7635/19	Santa Claus, LE 2000-1985						75	75	75			125	138
7635/28	Santa Claus, LE 1200-1984/2000-1985				95	95	100	100				155	171
7851/25	Doll, Madi			36								65	70
7871/28	Doll, Marion			43	43							80	86
7872/28	Doll, Marc			43	43							80	86
7873/28	Doll, Tanja			43	43							80	86
7874/28	Doll, Michael			43								80	86
7875/28	Doll, Yvonne			43								80	86
7892/40	Doll, Punch			56								100	108

Puppe 50/2/87, 9253/50 $395.

Santa Claus, 7635/19, L.E. 2000 pieces, 1985-1987, $138.

Animals of the Wild

Animals of the Wild

Steiff #	Description	80-81	81-82	82-83	83-84	84-85	85-86	86	87	88	89	90	Current
0020/11	Chimp, mhr	9	10	13	15	19	19	20	25	30	30	30	39
0020/13	Chimp, Mini Mohair										50	50	54
0020/16	Chimp, mhr	15	18									90	95
0020/25	Chimp	27	33									68	75
0020/35	Chimp	42	50									90	99
0020/50	Chimp	90	110									180	198
0020/60	Chimp	115	138									235	259
0021/17	Chimp, Mini Mohair									80		80	87
0022/16	Chimp			19								35	39
0022/26	Chimp			37	39	39	39	41	50	80	80	51	55
0022/36	Chimp			54	57	57	57	60	73	115	115	75	77
0022/52	Chimp			115	115	115	115	125	150	215		130	135
0025/23	Mungo, Brown	57	64	65								110	120
0026/23	Mungo, Yellow	57	64	65	65							110	120
0030/35	Orang, Baby	75	85									135	151
0035/35	Gorilla, Baby	75	85									135	151
0040/28	Gibbon, Baby	40	45	46	46	46	46	49	60	85	85	85	95
0040/45	Young Gibbon	64	72									165	185

Leopard, Standing, 6321/99 (60") 1980-1986, $1300.

Animals of the Wild

Steiff #	Description	80-81	81-82	82-83	83-84	84-85	85-86	86	87	88	89	90	Current
0040/60	Dangling Beige	116	140	145	145	145	145	155	185			240	269
0045/50	Monkey, Dressed	119	130	135	135							260	291
0079/03	Tree Pavian, Baby	57	64									110	123
0079/05	Tree Pavian, Stand St 24"	360	360	360								595	625
0080/08	Felt Elephant, 1880, 2 yr LE					60	60	60	60	60	60	75	83
0105/17	Penguin with Leather Wings, LE 8000						70	75	75	80	80	155	171
0111/21	Lying Lion, mhr, LE 2000					79	80	85				167	185
0111/35	Lying Lion, mhr, LE 1000					120	125	135	135			265	294
0112/17	Tiger, Lying, mhr, LE 2000				65	68	68	68	68			142	158
0112/28	Tiger, Lying, mhr, LE 2000				90	95	95	95				200	222
0117/18	Brown Reindeer, mhr, LE 4000											100	125
0123/19	Lion w/Tuba, LE									125	125	135	149
0124/19	Crocodile w/Trumpet, LE									125	125	135	149
0125/24	Jumbo Elephant, Mechanical, mhr, LE									300	300	300	330
0143/19	Chimp w/Unicycle, cover w/mhr, LE									125	125	135	138
0144/19	Gorilla Strong Man, mhr, LE 5000										125	125	138
0145/19	Elephant Balloon Seller, mhr, LE									135	135	135	149
0146/19	Hippo Fat Lady, mhr, LE									135	135	135	149
0147/12	Seal w/Ball, Stand, mhr, LE									100	100	100	109
0333/33	Molly Elephant, Sitting									185	185	185	200
0343/80	Super Molly Seal	225	270	275	275							390	429
0344/99	S Molly Elephant					600	600	650				900	972
0345/50	Molly Lynx	140	175									230	253
0368/45	Molly Baby Lion									195	125	135	
0370/30	Molly Leo Lion						70	85	125	135	87	94	
0370/70	Molly Leo Lion							295	400	400	250	270	
0371/30	Molly Baby Lion										110	119	
0375/45	Lion		175	180	180	180	180	195			342	369	
0376/45	Molly Young Tiger									195	125	135	
0376/60	Molly Young Tiger								330	330	356		
0378/60	Molly Tiger							230	230	230	248		
0380/30	Molly Tiger Taky						70	85	125	135	87	94	
0381/25	Bagheera Panther	48	53	53								225	248
0381/50	Super Molly Lion, Standing							280	380	380	380	410	
0382/22	Baby Hathi Elephant	43	48									225	248
0382/60	Super Molly Lion, Lying							260	360	360	360	389	
0383/22	King Louis Chimp	48	53	53								225	248
0385/75	Molly Puma					130	130			250		250	280
0385/98	Molly Puma					295						445	465
0387/75	Molly Panther					130	130	140	170	250	250	250	280
0387/98	Molly Panther						295	310				445	465
0390/40	Molly Leopard									160	160	105	113
0390/50	Molly Leopard							175	235	235	235	254	
0405/40	Molly Camel									230	230	125	135
0405/60	Molly Camel								315	315	315	340	
0411/40	Molly Zebra									125	125	125	135
0420/40	Molly Moose										230	145	157
0500/30	Bamboo Monkey, Light Brown							80	110		110	119	
0500/45	Bamboo Monkey, Light Brown							110	150		150	162	
0500/55	Bamboo Monkey, Light Brown							175	240		240	259	
0505/18	Elephant	38	42	43	43							75	83
0505/30	Bamboo Monkey, Cream							80	110		110	119	
0505/45	Bamboo Monkey, Cream							110	150		150	162	
0505/55	Bamboo Monkey, Cream							175	240		240	259	
0520/50	Bongo Orang., Rust							185	250	250	250	270	
0525/50	Bongo Orang., Cream							185	250	250	250	270	
0535/32	Baby Gorilla											81	87
0540/45	Gora Gorilla							185	250	250	150	162	
0540/60	Gora Gorilla							250	330	330	185	200	
0544/99	Gora Gorilla									1800	2000	2200	
0595/35	Mammouth, Trampy											105	113
0609/16	Camel, Standing St 63"	2385	2495	2700	2778	2778		3334		4315	3895	4000	
0710/35	Kangaroo/Baby	45	50	53	57	57	57	60				85	94
0755/28	Giraffe	30	39	39	39	45	45	48				60	66
0755/40	Giraffe	42	50	51	52	56	56	59				80	88
0755/60	Giraffe	70	89	90	90	90	90					135	149
0759/15	Giraffe St 60", mhr	1377	1450	1557	1557	1557	1557		1945		2593	2350	2400
0759/24	Giraffe St 96", mhr	2340	2500	2655	2655	2655	2655		3334		4769	4350	4600
0800/20	Lion	38	42									75	83

Animals of the Wild

Steiff #	Description	80-81	81-82	82-83	83-84	84-85	85-86	86	87	88	89	90	Current
0805/18	Lion, Standing	28										54	59
0805/26	Lion, Standing	39	48									75	83
0805/99	Lion, Standing										5694	6000	6500
0807/99	Lioness, Lying										3750	4000	4500
0809/11	Lion, Standing St 42"	2223	2547	2547	2547	2547	2547		2621			4300	4400
0812/16	Rango Lion	38	43	43	43							75	83
0815/15	Sulla Lioness	35	39	40								70	77
0820/16	Wittie Tiger	35	39	40	40							70	77
0822/99	Tiger, Standing St 59"	1800	2000	2210	2210	2210	2210		2778			3975	4100
0825/16	Sigi Leopard	35	39	40	40							70	77
0870/60	Tiger Cub "Pascha"					155	155	165	1100	265	265	265	286
0885/50	Leopard, Lying			105	105	105	105					195	211
0890/40	Leopard Cub	140	160	165	165							295	325
0892/40	Kango Kangaroo with Baby										210	140	151
1150/45	Seal Robby											96	104
1170/16	Walrus									65	65	42	45
1172/80	Walrus									375	375	375	405
1172/99	Walrus									1600	1600	1600	1728
1174/55	Walrus									215		215	232
1175/14	Seal	31	35	36	36	36	36					60	66
1175/20	Seal	49	59	60								95	105
1178/14	Seal	31	38	38	38	38	38					60	66
1179/04	Sealion Cub	125	140	145								235	259
1305/09	"Jumbo" Elephant, Mini-Mohair										50	50	54
1305/12	"Jumbo" Elephant, Mini-Mohair										70	70	76
1448/13	Kango Kangaroo										50	50	54

(Left) Chimp, Mini, 0021/17, 1989-1990, $87. (Middle) Chimp, Mini, 0020/13, 1989-1990, $54. (Right) Chimp, 0022/26, 1982-1990, $55.

Giraffe St., 0759/15, 60" high, 1980-1987, 1989-1990, $2400.

Animals of the Wild

Steiff #	Description	80-81	81-82	82-83	83-84	84-85	85-86	86	87	88	89	90	Current
1450/12	Jumbo Elephant	17	20	21	23	29						39	43
1451/09	Rhino	16	18	19	19							39	43
1451/12	Jumbo Elephant						23	24	30	50	50	32	35
1453/14	Hockey Dromedary	17	20	21	23							39	43
1453/15	Trampy Camel						23	24	30	50		50	54
1456/09	Nosy Rhino						23	24	30	50		50	54
1457/14	Elk	25	28	28								60	66
1458/12	Bison	22	24	25								50	55
1460/13	Lion	17	20	21	23	31						39	43
1461/12	Leo Lion						23	24	30	50	50	32	35
1463/18	Gaty Crocodile						27	29	35	55	55	55	59
1468/10	Wild Boar	19	21	21	21	21	21	22	27	40		39	43
1472/07	Dolphin	11	14	14	14	14	14	15	18	30	30	30	33
1473/09	Seal	13	16	17	18	18	18	19	23	40	40	40	44
1474/10	Walrus	16	17	18	18	18						39	43
1512/16	Ossi, Zebra			25	26	26	26					48	52
2040/25	Putsi Otter, Standing								85	110		115	124
2045/25	Putsi Otter, Sitting								85	110		115	124
2160/20	"Otty" Otter			30								55	59
2251/18	Guinea Pig Ginny											37	40
2251/22	Guinea Pig Ginny											44	48
2270/25	Otter	32	32									65	72
2270/35	Otter	54										95	105
2300/10	Fish, Blue, mhr	8	9									40	47
2301/10	Fish, Gold, mhr	8	9									40	47
2311/25	Fish, Green	28										52	55
2320/25	Dolphin	23	26	27	27							44	46
2320/35	Dolphin	28	33	33	33							55	58
2322/35	Finny Dolphin								57	75		75	81
2322/50	Finny Dolphin								89	120		120	130
2322/99	Finny Dolphin								450	600		600	648
2505/12	Penguin	16	19	19	20	20	20	21	26	37	37	37	41
2505/27	Penguin	35	40	41								70	77
2505/40	Penguin	59	77									115	127
2507/20	Baby Penguin				33	33	33	35	42	70	70	70	76
2507/38	Penguin			72	72	72	72	76	92	135		130	140
2509/09	Penguin St 36"	450	450	450	450	450	450		620		834	850	875
2510/40	Charly Penguin								115	150	150	150	162
2511/26	Paddy Puffin	57	65									115	127
2531/13	Parakeet, Gold/Green	18	22	23	23	23	23					54	59
2534/13	Parakeet, White/Blue	18	22	23	23	23	23	25	30	47	47	47	52
2540/30	Parrot, Red, Studio	76	89	90	90	90	90		130			225	265
2541/30	Parrot, Blue, Studio	76	89	90	90	90	90		130			225	265
2544/30	Lora Parrot, Red								95	125		125	135
2545/30	Cockatoo			90	90	90						180	194
2550/30	Lora Parrot, Green								95	125		165	178
2555/14	Parrot Lori											45	49
2560/14	Tucan Tucky											45	49
2560/20	Tucky Tucan										105	105	113
2565/14	Pelican Peli											45	49
2565/20	Peli Pelican										105	105	113
2570/14	Penguin Peggy											45	49
2605/20	Kingfisher 8"	82	82									158	165
2606/50	Heron 20"	190	190	195	195	195						360	365
2608/50	Stork 20"	200	200	200	200	200						380	395
2612/20	Swan, White				40	40	40					75	81
2615/28	Falcon, Studio	85	97	99	99	99	99	105	125	195		200	220
2620/99	Peacock, Studio	800	950	1000	1000	1000	1000		1400	1600	1963	1700	2000
2621/80	Peacock, Studio	750	900	900	1000							1500	1600
2650/23	Young Wild Boar									120		120	130
2655/28	Young Wild Boar "Wutzi"											100	105
2655/40	Young Wild Boar "Wutzi"											135	143
2660/20	Bora Wild Boar								57	75		75	81
2660/30	Bora Wild Boar								89	120		120	130
2675/15	Wild Boar	33	39	39	39	39	39					65	72
2675/20	Wild Boar			50	52	65	65					90	97
2677/30	Baby Boar			81	81	81	81	86				140	151
2678/50	Wild Boar St		230	235	235	235						425	459
2690/32	Scottish Highland Bull									180	180	180	194

Animals of the Wild

Steiff #	Description	80-81	81-82	82-83	83-84	84-85	85-86	86	87	88	89	90	Current
2695/35	Buffalo									200	200	200	216
2897/30	Jr. Leo Lion Cub			91	95	95	95	100	100	180	180	180	194
2912/18	Snuffy Elephant								50	65		65	70
2914/18	Snuffy Lion								55	75	75	75	81
3247/26	Swan	57	65	66								140	154
3475/40	Elbow Puppet-Leopard	74	80	82								140	168
3478/50	Elbow Puppet-Puma/Lion	86	94									170	204
3518/14	Snuffy Lion	19	24	24								38	42
3518/18	Snuffy Lion	25	32	32								50	55
5322/35	Panther, Lying	58	75									110	121
5322/50	Panther, Lying	98										180	198
5340/33	Cosy Elephant, Lying									120		120	130
5350/15	Cosy Jumbo Elephant				39	39	41	52	70	70	70	76
5350/22	Cosy Jumbo Elephant				60	60	64	80	110		110	123
5350/30	Cosy Jumbo Elephant					100	100					165	178
5351/40	Leopard, Lying	76	84	85								140	154
5352/25	Cosy Elephant			58	58							95	103
5370/28	Cosy Panther	57	63	63	63	63	63	67	82	110		110	121
5372/33	Cosy Puma		64	65	65	65	65					120	130
5374/17	Cosy Seal					25	25	27	33	45		45	49
5374/35	Cosy Seal			49	49	49	49	52	63	90		90	97
5375/30	Cosy Seal "Robby", Grey							45	58	85		85	92
5375/31	Cosy Seal "Robby", Beige							45	58	85		85	92
5375/57	Cosy Seal			81	81	81	81					145	157
5376/50	Cosy Seal		125	126								230	248
5387/27	Cosy Whale				27	27	27	29	36	55		45	49
5410/80	Cosy Dolphin		157									250	270
5420/19	Cosy Nosy Rhino, Lying									95		95	103
5420/75	Cosy Nosy Rhino, Lying									300		300	324
5420/99	Cosy Nosy Rhino, Lying									1600		1600	1728
5422/20	Cosy Nosy Rhino, Standing									95		95	103
5422/40	Cosy Nosy Rhino, Standing									150		150	162
5438/25	Dolphin "Finny", Ice Blue									53		53	57
5450/27	Cosy Gora Monkey		79	80	80							145	157
5578/11	Penquin								23	30		32	35
5585/15	Blue Dolphin								23	35		35	38
5588/15	Grey Dolphin								23	35		35	38
5655/16	Mini Floppy Elephant										53	53	57
5706/20	Kiddi Elephant										75	75	81
5710/20	Elephant	45										80	88
5710/30	Elephant	61	66									110	121
5715/20	Cocki	41	44	45								75	83
5715/30	Cocki	59	65									110	121
5810/22	Elephant	43	48	49	49	49						79	87
6190/30	Chimp	38	47									75	83
6215/28	Possy Guenon Monkey										120	120	130
6220/28	Possy Elephant										125	125	135
6228/28	Possy Lion										120	120	130
6240/20	Toldi Chimp			25	28							46	50
6240/30	Toldi Chimp			49	53							90	97
6271/27	Toldi Elephant									85		85	92
6272/27	Toldi Monkey									80		80	86
6280/70	Dangling Monkey											240	254
6285/55	Lulac Tiger			125	125	125	125					235	254
6288/32	Dangling Monkey "Mungo"							60	72			110	119
6304/50	Hippo	170										300	330
6305/50	Rhino	170										300	330
6310/60	Bison	175	195	200	200	200						325	358
6314/60	Tiger	138	150	155	155							270	297
6315/30	Puma, Lying	75	75									145	155
6315/40	Puma, Standing	80	87									155	175
6315/99	Puma, Lying	375		425	425	425						750	850
6316/99	Puma, Sitting	590		700	700	700						1100	1300
6320/30	Leopard, Lying	75	82									145	155
6320/40	Leopard, Standing	80	80									155	175
6320/99	Leopard, Lying	375	415	425	425	425	425					750	800
6321/99	Leopard, Standing	590	650	675	675	675	675					1100	1300
6322/99	Leopard, Sitting St	695	713	700	700	700	700					1300	1400
6323/99	Panther, Lying	375	415	425	425	425						750	850

Animals of the Wild

Steiff #	Description	80-81	81-82	82-83	83-84	84-85	85-86	86	87	88	89	90	Current
6325/99	Panther, Standing	590	650	675	675	675						1100	1300
6460/27	Chimpanzee (Hand Puppet)	26	28	28	28	28	28	30	36			50	56
6471/27	Lion (Hand Puppet)	33	36	37	37	37	37	39	47			62	69
6474/27	Wolf (Hand Puppet)	33	36									62	69
6476/27	Crocodile (Hand Puppet)	33	36									62	69
6488/32	Happy Guenon Monkey										105	105	113
6820/18	Lion (Hand Puppet), mhr	23										90	101
6880/17	Tiger (Hand Puppet), mhr	23										90	101
6991/30	Chimpanzee (Hand Puppet)	46	50	51	51	51	51	54	65			85	95
7086/10	Wool Bird Assmt	10	10									16	18
7116/08	Birds, Assmt	5	7	7	7							11	12
7276/09	Fish, Assmt	10	11									19	21
7390/10	Penquin	8	10									15	17
7500/05	Pitty Elephant	6	7									9	10
7501/05	Pitty Lion	6	7									9	10

Chimp with Unicycle, cover, 0143/19, L.E., 1989-1990, $138. (Unicycle is not present.)

Jumbo Elephant, Mechanical, 0125/24, L.E., 1988-1990, $330.

0112,28
Lying Tiger

0112,17
Lying Tiger

Left: Wild Boar Baby, 2678/55, Studio, 1981-1985, $459. *Photograph courtesy Margarete Steiff GmbH.*

(Left) Lying Tiger, 0112/28, L.E., 1983-1987, $222. (Right) Lying Tiger, 0112/17, L.E. 2000 pieces, 1983-1987, $158. *Photograph courtesy Margarete Steiff GmbH and Reeves International.*

Numerical Listing

Steiff #	Description	80-81	81-82	82-83	83-84	84-85	85-86	86	87	88	89	90	Current
0020/11	Chimp, mhr	9	10	13	15	19	19	20	25	30	30	30	39
0020/13	Chimp, Mini Mohair										50	50	54
0020/16	Chimp, mhr	15	18									90	95
0020/25	Chimp	27	33									68	75
0020/35	Chimp	42	50									90	99
0020/50	Chimp	90	110									180	198
0020/60	Chimp	115	138									235	259
00206	Teddy Donald, Walt Disney World, 6th convention, 1993, Offered at $275												395
0021/17	Chimp, Mini Mohair										80	80	87
0022/16	Chimp			19								35	39
0022/26	Chimp			37	39	39	39	41	50	80	80	51	55
0022/36	Chimp			54	57	57	57	60	73	115	115	75	77
0022/52	Chimp			115	115	115	115	125	150	215		130	135
0025/23	Mungo, Brown	57	64	65								110	120
0026/23	Mungo, Yellow	57	64	65	65							110	120
0030/35	Orang, Baby	75	85									135	151
0035/35	Gorilla, Baby	75	85									135	151
0040/28	Gibbon, Baby	40	45	46	46	46	46	49	60	85	85	85	95
0040/45	Young Gibbon	64	72									165	185
0040/60	Dangling Beige	116	140	145	145	145	145	155	185			240	269
0045/50	Monkey, Dressed	119	130	135	135							260	291
0050/28	Dinosaur, 1959, LE 4000											200	220
0055/00	Eric Bat Set, 2 pc., 1960, LE 4000											200	220
0079/03	Tree Pavian, Baby	57	64									110	123
0079/05	Tree Pavian, Stand St 24"	360	360	360								595	625
0080/08	Felt Elephant, 1880, 2 yr LE				60	60	60	60	60	60		75	83
0081/14	Felt Duck, 1892 Rep., LE 4000									125	125	125	138
0082/20	Roly Poly Bear, 1894, 2 yr LE				69	70	70	70		80	80	95	105
0085/12	Bear on Wheels, LE 12,000					95	100	100		120	120	165	182
0090/11	Polar Bear Jntd Legs/Rtng Head, LE 3000							95		95		155	265
0091/14	Pig, Univ Head Movement, 1909, LE 4000										155	155	171
0093/12	Fox, 1910, LE 4000										150	150	165
0095/17	Begging Rabbit 7x Jntd 1911, LE 4000									145	145	145	165
0100/86	Elephant on Wheels w/Circus Calp., LE						2100	2100		2100		1200	1320
0100/87	Circus Cage w/Lying Lion, LE									275		550	605
0100/88	Circus Wagon w/Giraffe, LE										325	450	495
0100/89	Circus Wagon w/Tiger, LE										350	550	605
0100/90	Circus Wagon w/Two Bears, LE											450	495
0101/14	Bully Dog, 1927 Rep., LE 6000							75	75	120		145	160
0104/10	Tabby Cat, 1928 Rep., LE 6000							75	75	120		130	143
0105/17	Penguin with Leather Wings, LE 8000						70	75	75	80	80	155	171
0108/14	Drinking Cat, 1933, LE 4000											185	204
0111/21	Lying Lion, mhr, LE 2000				79	80	85					167	185
0111/35	Lying Lion, mhr, LE 1000				120	125	135	135				265	294
0112/17	Tiger, Lying, mhr, LE 2000			65	68	68	68	68				142	158
0112/28	Tiger, Lying, mhr, LE 2000			90	95	95	95					200	222
0115/18	Roly Poly Bear w/Rattle 1908, mhr, LE									125	125	125	138
0116/25	Record Teddy, 1913, LE 4000											300	330
0116/28	Roly Poly Clown w/Rattle 1909, mhr, LE									260	260	260	280
0117/18	Brown Reindeer, mhr, LE 4000											100	125
0118/00	Sleigh Set, mhr, LE 6000										275	275	320
0118/25	Boxer, Lying, mhr, LE 2000				55	57	57	57	57			85	151
011863	Black Margaret Strong Bear with white bib, (referred to as Minnie Bear), Walt Disney World, 5th Convention, LE 1500, 1992, Offered at $200												425 up
011979	Teddile, The Toy Store, 1992, LE 2000 announced, 1000 produced												125
011986	Light Grey Bear, Disneyland Convention, Anaheim, California, LE 1500, 1992, Offered at $275												325 up
0120/19	Bear Band Leader w/Baton, LE									125	125	135	165 up
0121/19	Dog w/Trombone, LE									125	125	135	149

Continued on Page 92

Numerical Listing

Steiff #	Description	80-81	81-82	82-83	83-84	84-85	85-86	86	87	88	89	90	Current
0122/19	Cat w/Drum, LE									125	125	135	149
0123/19	Lion w/Tuba, LE									125	125	135	149
0124/19	Crocodile w/Trumpet, LE									125	125	135	149
0125/24	Jumbo Elephant, Mechanical, mhr, LE									300	300	300	330
0126/20	Donkey Mechanical 1909 Rep, LE									185	185	185	204
0130/17	Unicorn, Lying, LE 2000				40	42						135	151
0130/27	Unicorn, Lying, LE 2000			55	57							175	196
0130/28	Bear on 4 Legs, Univ. Head Mov., mhr, LE 4000										400	400	465
0131/00	Three Bears in a Tub, LE 1800							275	275			310	375
0132/24	"Wiwag" Seesaw P-Toy w/Two Bears, mhr, LE									260	260	260	286
0134/22	Niki Rabbit, mhr					58						155	185
0134/28	Niki Rabbit, mhr				70	75						195	211
0135/20	Baby Bear Pull Toy, cover w/mhr, LE 4000									275	275		303
0143/19	Chimp w/Unicycle, cover w/mhr, LE										125	125	138
0144/19	Gorilla Strong Man, mhr, LE 5000											125	138
0145/12	Lamb							30	30			30	32
0145/19	Elephant Balloon Seller, mhr, LE										135	135	149
0146/13	Cat, Crouching							50	50	50		50	54
0146/19	Hippo Fat Lady, mhr, LE									135	135		149
0147/12	Seal w/Ball, Stand, mhr, LE									100	100		109
0147/20	Rabbit, Begging							50	50			50	54
0148/03	Teddy Bear Pin				9							15	20
0149/19	Fire Eater Dragon, mhr, LE 5000											125	138
0150/32	Richard Steiff 1902-1903 Bear, LE				90	100						285	350

(Left) Baby Elephant Balloon Seller, 0145/19, L.E., 1989-1990, $149. (Right) Jumbo Elephant, Mini, 1305/12, 1989-1990, $76.

Right: (Left) Donkey, Mechanical, 0126/20, Replica 1909, L.E., 1988-1990, $204. (Right) Jumbo Elephant, Mechanical, 0125/24, 1988-1990, $330.

Below: (Left) Unicorn, Lying, 0130/17, L.E. 2000 pieces, 1983-1985, $151. (Right) Unicorn, Lying, 0130/27, L.E. 2000 pieces, 1983-1985, $196. *Photograph courtesy Margarete Steiff GmbH and Reeves International.*

0130,17 Lying Unicorn

0130,27 Lying Unicorn

Numerical Listing

Steiff #	Description	80-81	81-82	82-83	83-84	84-85	85-86	86	87	88	89	90	Current
0151/25	1904 Cinnamon Bear, mhr, LE					70	75	79				165	190
0151/32	1904 Cinnamon Bear, mhr, LE					85	90	95				265	325
0151/40	1904 Cinnamon Bear, mhr, LE					125	135	145				435	525
0152/25	Mr. Vanilla, Hobby Center Toys, LE 1000										**		335
0153/43	100th Anniv. L.E. Original Teddy	150										800	935
0155/00	Hoppy Rabbit Set, 3pc. 1984, LE					150	150	150				265	292
0155/15	Baby Bear in Christening Outfit, LE						60	75	75			99	109
0155/22E	Santa's Elf, LE									100	100	125	138
0155/22	Flower Bearer, L.E. 2000 pc.					75	80	100	100			125	140
0155/23	Ring Bearer, L.E. 2000 pc.					75	80	100	100			125	140
0155/26	Margaret Strong Bear, mhr, LE			48	48	50	53	56	69	100	100	100	110
0155/32	Margaret Strong Bear, mhr, LE			62	62	65	69	73	89	135	135	135	142
0155/34	Victorian Girl Bear 1986, LE 1200						125					225	248
0155/35	Victorian Boy Bear 1986, LE 1200						125	125				225	248
0155/36	Bride, L.E. 2000, 1984					100	110	125	150	200	200	215	241
0155/37	Groom, L.E. 2000, 1984					100	110	125	150	200	200	215	241
0155/38	Anniv. Ltd/Mother/Baby, mhr, 7500		150									495	585
0155/38	Santa Bear, 1000 pc., 1986							125	150	200	200	200	220
0155/42	Margaret Strong Bear, mhr, LE				90	95	100	105	125	200	200	200	240
0155/51	Margaret Strong Gold Bear, mhr, LE					185	195	205	250	350	350	350	389
0155/60	Margaret Strong Gold Bear, mhr, LE					250	285	300	375	495	495	495	549
0156/00	Margaret Strong Cinnamon Bear Set, mhr, LE					300	300					590	680
0156/26	Cinnamon Bear, mhr, LE							53				100	115
0156/32	Cinnamon Bear, mhr							69				135	155
0156/34	M. Strong Captain Strong, LE									200	200	215	237
0156/36	M. Strong Victorian Lady, LE								150	150	150	195	215
0156/37	M. Strong Victorian Man, LE								150	150	150	195	215
0156/38	Vic. Santa Bxd, 1200 pc., 1987								150	200	200	200	210
0156/42	Cinnamon Bear, mhr, LE							100				195	224
0157/26	Margaret Strong Cream Bear, mhr, LE					50	53	56				145	161
0157/32	Margaret Strong Cream Bear, mhr, LE					65	69	73				185	205
0157/42	Margaret Strong Cream Bear, mhr, LE					95	100	105				265	294
0157/51	Margaret Strong Cream Bear, mhr, LE						195	205				565	625
0157/60	Margaret Strong Cream Bear, mhr, LE						285	300				625	975
0158/17	Snap-Apart Bear, mhr, LE 5000										135	275	325
0158/25	White Bear, Leather Paws, mhr, LE					60	60	60				165	195
0158/31	White Bear, Leather Paws, mhr, LE					79	79	79				255	325
0158/41	White Bear, Leather Paws, mhr, LE					110	110	110				325	438
0158/50	White Bear, Leather Paws, mhr, LE						225					1200	1535
0160/00	M. Strong Choc. Brown Set, 4 pc.			275								480	585
0162/00	"The Birthplace of the Teddy," LE, 1984					150	159	159	159			260	300
0163/19	Bear Drsd as Clown, White Tag								50			195	220
0163/19	Bear Drsd as Clown, Yellow Tag								50			125	155
0163/20	Clown Teddy, mhr, LE 5000										100	100	110
0164/29	Somersault Bear, mhr, LE 5000											395	410
0164/30	Odd Yellow Dolly Bear, 471 pc.							135				245	295
0164/31	Circus Dolly Bear/Yellow, mhr, LE 2000 white tag							135	175	175		185	204
0164/32	Circus Dolly Bear/Green, mhr, LE 2000 white tag							135	175	175		185	204
0164/34	Circus Dolly Bear/Violet, mhr, LE 2000 white tag							135	175	175		185	204
0165/28	1909 Gold Teddy, mhr, LE					55	59	62	62			75	100
0165/38	1909 Gold Teddy Bear, mhr, LE				80	85	90	95				110	165
0165/51	1909 Gold Teddy, mhr, LE					150	159	169				435	487
0165/60	1909 Gold Teddy, mhr, LE						275	290	290			580	680
0166/25	Blond Teddy, 1909, mhr, LE									100	100	100	109
0166/35	Blond Teddy, 1909, mhr, LE									145	145	145	160
0166/43	Blond Teddy, 1909, mhr, LE									225	225	225	248
0167/22	Giengen Bear, Grey, 1906 Rep, mhr, LE						55	69	100	100	100		109
0167/32	Giengen Bear, Grey, mhr, LE						85	90	100	160	160	160	176
0167/42	Giengen Bear, Grey, mhr, LE						120	125	150	225	225	225	350
0167/52	Giengen Bear, Grey, 1906 Rep, mhr, LE							195	250	350	350	350	500
0168/22	Giengen Bear, Beige, 1906 Rep, mhr, LE							55	69	100	100	100	109
0168/42	Giengen Bear, Beige, 1906 Rep, mhr, LE							125	150	225		235	259
0169/65	Teddy Bear, Grey/Brown Tipped, 1926, mhr, LE 5000											525	595
0170/32	Teddy Clown 1926 Rep, LE 10,000							150	150			395	435
0171/25	Teddy Rose, LE											195	235
0171/41	Teddy Rose w/Ctr. Seam, LE 10,000								1100	300	230	345	350
0172/18	Dicky Mauve, Hobby Center Toys, 1991, LE 2000												275
0172/32	Dicky Bear, LE 20,000, 1985						100	105	105	125		225	275
0173/40	Black Bear, 1907 Rep, LE									300	300	600	535

Steiff #	Description	80-81	81-82	82-83	83-84	84-85	85-86	86	87	88	89	90	Current
0174/35	Muzzle Bear, White, 1908, mhr, LE 6000											295	340
0174/46	Muzzle Bear, White, 1908 Rep, mhr, LE 5000									375	375	375	390
0174/60	Muzzle Bear, White, 1908, mhr, LE 2650									500	500		550
0175/19	Teddy Baby Ringmaster, mhr, LE									140	140		154
0175/29	Teddy Baby, Brown, mhr, LE					85	95	100	125	175	175	175	193
0175/35	Teddy Baby, Brown, mhr, LE					110	125	135	165	225	225	225	247
0175/42	Teddy Baby, Brown, mhr, LE					165	175	185	235	300	300	300	330
0176/29	Teddy Baby, Tan, mhr, LE						95	100				245	270
0176/35	Teddy Baby, Tan, mhr, LE						125	135	135			265	292
0176/42	Teddy Baby, Tan, mhr, LE						175	185				400	440
0177/19	Teddy Baby Food Vendor, mhr, LE 5000											140	154
0178/29	1938 Panda, mhr, LE					85	85					265	265
0178/35	1938 Panda, mhr, LE					110	110					320	320
0179/19	Dicky Rose, Hobby Center Toys, LE 2000											**	350
0180/50	Petsy Bear, Ctr. Seam Bicolor, mhr, LE 5000										375	375	425
0181/35	Petsy Bear, Ctr Seam Brass, mhr, LE 5000										225	225	235
0190/17	"Jackie" Bear Tub, 1953, mhr, LE 12,000										135	135	175
0190/25	Teddy "Jackie" 1953 Rep, mhr, LE 10,000						110	135				295	325
0190/35	"Jackie" Bear, 1953 Rep, mhr, LE 4000									300	300	300	395
0201/10	Beige Teddy Bear, Jointed, mhr, LE					35	36					88	95
0201/11	Original Teddy, Beige, mhr	9	10	13	15	19	20	21	25	30	30	30	35
0201/14	Beige Teddy Bear, Jointed, mhr, LE			25		30	30					75	81
0201/18	Original Teddy, Beige, mhr				30	35	37	39	47	70	70	70	84
0201/26	Original Teddy, Beige, mhr	27	30	33	36	40	43	45	55	85	85	85	98
0201/36	Original Teddy, Beige, mhr	36	40	48	50	55	59	62	75	115	115	115	132
0201/41	Original Teddy Bear, Beige, mhr			70	75	75	79	85	100	160	160	160	165
0201/51	Original Teddy Bear, Beige, mhr			115	120	120	125	135	165	250	250	250	275
0201/75	Original Teddy Bear, Beige, mhr				450	500	529	560	675	975	975	975	980
0201/99	Original Bear Beige, mhr			700	700	750	795	850	9100	1450		2300	2500
0202/10	Caramel Teddy Bear, Jointed, mhr, LE					35	36					88	95
0202/11	Original Teddy, Caramel, mhr	9	10	13	15	19	20	21	25	30	30	30	35
0202/12	Original Teddy, Caramel, Mini-Mohair										50	50	54
0202/14	Caramel Teddy Bear, Jointed, mhr, LE			25		30	30					75	81
0202/15	Original Teddy, Caramel, Mini-Mohair										70	70	76
0202/18	Original Teddy, Caramel, mhr				30	35	37	39	47	70	70	70	84
0202/26	Original Teddy, Caramel, mhr	27	30	33	36	40	43	45	55	85	85	85	98
0202/36	Original Teddy, Caramel, mhr	36	40	48	50	55	59	62	75	115	115	115	132
0202/41	Original Teddy, Caramel, mhr	53	60	70	75	75	79	85	100	160	160	160	184
0202/51	Original Teddy, Caramel, mhr	84	100	115	120	120	125	135	165	250	250	250	288
0202/75	Original Teddy, Caramel, mhr				450	500	529	560	675	975		1195	1434
0202/99	Original Teddy, Caramel, mhr				700	750	795	850	9100	1450		2300	2760
0203/00	White Orig. Bears w/Paws, 5 pc.											625	775
0203/10	White Teddy Bear, Jointed, mhr, LE					35	36					88	95
0203/11	Original Teddy Bear, White, mhr			13	15	19	20	21	25			39	41
0203/14	White Teddy Bear, Jointed, mhr, LE			25		30	30	30	30			75	81
0203/18	Original Teddy White, mhr				30	35	37	39	47			87	104
0203/26	Original Teddy Bear, White, mhr			33	36	40	43	45	55			110	115
0203/36	Original Teddy Bear, White, mhr			48	50	55	59	62	75			175	180
0203/41	Original Teddy Bear, White, mhr			70	75	75	79	85	100			235	240
0203/51	Original Teddy Bear, White, mhr				120	120	125	135	165			310	372
0203/75	Original Teddy Bear, White, mhr				450	500						1250	1500
0203/99	Original Teddy Bear, White, mhr				700	750						2800	3360
0204/16	1982 "The Teddy Tea Party," LE 10,000			175								300	385
0205/26	Original Teddy, Caramel	32	35	37	37	45	45	48	58			80	86
0205/35	Original Teddy, Caramel	45	50	52	54	62	62	66	80			110	119
0205/50	Original Teddy, Caramel	97	105	120	120	120						235	254
0206/10	Chocolate Teddy Bear, Jointed, mhr, LE					35	36					88	95
0206/11	Original Teddy, Choc. Brown, mhr					19	20	21	25	30	30	30	35
0206/14	Chocolate Teddy Bear, Jointed, mhr, LE					30	30	30				75	81
0206/18	Original Teddy, Chocolate Brown, mhr					35	37	39	47	70	70	70	78
0206/26	Original Teddy, Chocolate Brown, mhr					40	43	45	55	85	85	85	95
0206/36	Original Teddy, Chocolate Brown, mhr					55	59	62	75	115	115	115	129
0206/41	Original Teddy, Chocolate Brown, mhr					75	79	85	100	160	160	160	179
0206/51	Original Teddy, Chocolate Brown, mhr					120	125	135	165	250	250	250	280
0207/10	Grey Teddy Bear, mhr, LE						36	38	38			88	95
0207/12	Original Teddy, Grey, mhr											50	54
0207/14	Grey Teddy Bear, mhr, LE						30					75	81
0207/15	Original Teddy, Grey, mhr											70	76
0207/26	Original Teddy, Grey, mhr, LE							45	45	85	85	85	98

Continued on Page 96

Hippo Fat Lady, 0146/19,
L.E., 1989-1990, $149.

Camel, Standing, 0609/16, Studio, 63", 1980-
1985, $4000. *Photograph courtesy of Margarete
Steiff GmbH.*

"Tyros" Tyrannosaur, 0051/20, L.E., 1991, $250.

(Left) Dolphin "Clippy," 1472/07, 1980-1990, $33. (Right) Seal with Ball, Stand, 0147/12, L.E., 1989-1990, $109.

Numerical Listing

Steiff #	Description	80-81	81-82	82-83	83-84	84-85	85-86	86	87	88	89	90	Current
0207/36	Original Teddy, Grey, mhr, LE							62	62	115	115	115	132
0207/41	Original Teddy, Grey, mhr, LE							85	85	160	160	160	184
0208/10	Black Teddy Bear, mhr, LE				36		38	38				88	95
0208/14	Black Teddy Bear, mhr, LE				30							75	81
0209/12	Original Teddy, Black, mhr											50	54
0209/15	Original Teddy, Black, mhr											70	76
0210/12	Original Teddy, Blond, Mini-Mohair										50	50	54
0210/15	Original Teddy, Blond, Mini-Mohair										70	70	76
0210/22	Teddy Roosevelt Comm. Set, mhr, LE			1100								275	325
0211/10	Original Teddy, Rose, LE 8000											60	64
0211/12	Original Teddy, Rose, mhr											50	54
0211/15	Original Teddy, Rose, mhr											70	76
0211/26	Luv Bear-er, mhr					45	48					135	151
0211/36	Luv Bear-er, mhr					60	64					175	196
0212/10	Original Teddy, Cream, mhr, LE							38	38			82	90
0213/10	Original Teddy, Cinnamon, mhr, LE							38	38			82	90
0214/10	Original Teddy, Gold, mhr, LE							38	38			82	90
0215/35	Dormy Bear	60	67	68	68							150	162
0217/34	Dorma Bear		65	66	66	66	66	70				145	149
0218/14	Panda, Hobby Center Toys, mhr, LE 1000									**			350
0218/16	Bear		28	28	28	28						60	62
0220/30	Orsi Bear	48	54	55	55							120	130
0223/30	Bruno Bear, Jointed, mhr, LE			60	60	62	62	62				135	149
0224/35	Petsy Soft											93	100
0225/27	Baby Ophelia with Tutu, mhr, LE								140	140	140		154
0225/42	Ophelia Bear, Jointed, mhr, LE					150	159	169	1100	275	275	275	320
0226/28	Growling Bear											100	107
0227/33	Schnuffy Bear Dressed, 1907 Rep, mhr, LE							1100	275	275			303
0228/33	Growling Bear, mhr							90	125	125	125		137
0228/38	Growling Bear, mhr							125	165	165	165		182
0228/48	Growling Bear, mhr							195	250	250	250		275
0230/20	Teddy Petsy, Rust					39	39					69	74
0230/28	Teddy Petsy, Rust					50	50	53	64	95	95	63	68
0230/35	Teddy Petsy, Rust					70	70	75	90	130	130	85	92
0230/45	Teddy Petsy, Rust					100	100	105	140	190	190	120	130
0233/20	Teddy Petsy, Blonde					39	39	41	41			65	70
0233/28	Teddy Petsy, Blonde					50	50	53	65	95	95	63	68
0233/35	Teddy Petsy, Blonde					70	70	75	90	130	130	85	92
0233/45	Teddy Petsy, Blonde					100	100	105	140	190	190	120	130
0233/80	Teddy Petsy, Blonde						400	425	4100	4100		600	648
0235/20	Teddy Petsy, Cream					39	39	41	41			65	70
0235/28	Teddy Petsy, Cream					50	50	53	65	95	95	63	68
0235/35	Teddy Petsy, Cream					70	70	75	90	130	130	85	92
0235/45	Teddy Petsy, Cream					100	100	105	140	190	190	120	130
0236/28	Petsy Teddy, Augbergine											62	75
0237/20	S-Soft Teddy, Beige, Jointed, mhr, LE					40						90	97
0237/28	Petsy Teddy, Blackberry											62	75
0237/28	S-Soft Teddy, Beige, Jointed, mhr, LE					55	59	62	62			125	135
0237/35	S-Soft Teddy, Beige, Jointed, mhr, LE					75	79	85	85			165	178
0237/45	S-Soft Teddy, Beige, Jointed, mhr, LE					110	115	115	115			245	265
0238/35	Petsy Teddy											85	92
0240/28	Petsy Panda							60	72	110	110	68	73
0240/35	Petsy Panda							80	96	150	150	150	162
0240/45	Petsy Panda							115	140	200		200	216
0243/32	Gold Bear w/Red Ribbon, mhr, Walt Disney World, 1st Convention, LE 1000, only 500 produced.									95			400 up
0244/35	White Petsy Bear, Walt Disney World, 2nd Convention, LE 1000										115		325 up
0245/32	Grey Margaret Strong Bear, mhr, Walt Disney World, 3rd Convention, LE 1000											125	300 up
0245/40	Passport Bear, mhr, LE						110	115	140	210		225	240
0246/32	Black Margaret Strong Bear with Mickey Mouse Mask (referred to as Mickey Bear), 32cm, Walt Disney World, 4th Convention, LE 1500 1991, Offered at $175											450 up	
0251/34	Berlin Bear, mhr, LE						110	115	115			210	230
0255/35	Clifford Berryman Bear, mhr, LE								170	225	225		248
0270/28	Teddy Dressed as a Bride, mhr							100	125	175		180	198
0271/28	Teddy Dressed as a Groom, mhr							100	125			180	198

Steiff #	Description	80-81	81-82	82-83	83-84	84-85	85-86	86	87	88	89	90	Current
0275/28	Teddy Dressed with Dirndl, mhr							100	125	175		175	193
0276/28	Teddy Dressed with Lederhosen, mhr							100	125	175	175	175	193
0280/28	Teddy Dressed as a Sailor Boy, mhr							100	125	175	175	175	193
0281/28	Teddy Dressed as a Sailor Girl, mhr							100	125	175	175	175	193
0283/28	Teddy Dressed w/Black Forest Outfit, mhr								150	150		165	182
0284/28	Teddy Dressed w/Farmer Outfit, mhr								150	150		165	182
0290/32	Toddel	43	50	51								100	108
0302/30	Zotty	60	67	70	70	70	70					110	119
0302/40	Zotty	85	95	98	98	98	98					160	173
0302/50	Zotty	125	140	145	145	145	145	155				230	248
0305/22	Zotty	34	40	41								200	230
0305/30	Zotty Bear						63	67	81	135	135	85	92
0305/32	Zotty, mhr	46	50	55								270	311
0305/40	Zotty Bear						95	100	125	200	200	125	135
0305/45	Zotty, mhr	98	115	120								410	472
0305/50	Zotty Bear					130	140	170	250	250		150	162
0310/19	Buddha Bear, mhr				40	40	43					130	155
0312/30	Minky Zotty								135	135		89	96
0312/40	Minky Zotty								200	200		130	140
0312/50	Minky Zotty								250	250		155	167
0318/32	Molly Minky										115	77	83
0318/42	Molly Minky										160	160	173
0320/55	Molly Teddy		115	120								230	248
0320/65	Molly Teddy		160	165	165	165	165	175	210	265	265	165	178
0321/22	Molly Teddy, Champagne								65	65		42	45
0321/32	Molly Teddy, Champagne								115	115		70	76
0321/55	Molly Teddy, Champagne				100	100	100	105	140	200	200	125	138
0322/22	Molly Teddy, Cream								65	65		42	45
0322/32	Molly Teddy, Cream								115	115		70	74
0322/40	Molly Teddy, Cream					80	80	85	110	150	150	96	104
0323/50	Super Molly Teddy, Standing								395	525		539	582
0323/60	Molly Teddy, Brown											175	189
0323/65	Molly Panda		158	165	165							295	319
0324/60	Super Molly Teddy, Lying								395	525		525	567
0324/75	Molly Teddy											265	286
0326/32	Molly Panda, B/W	52	58	60	60	60	60	65	78	110	110	110	121
0326/45	Molly Panda, B/W	93	100	110	110	110	110	115	140	190		190	209
0327/32	Molly Panda, Brown	48	54									130	143
0327/45	Molly Panda, Brown	90	100									220	242
0327/85	Standing Bear on 4 Legs							2963		4335	3895	3995	
0328/99	Bear Standing on 2 Legs							2963		4335	3895	3995	
0329/08	Brown Bear Standing on 4 Legs							2315			2500	2900	
0329/16	Brown Bear Standing							2315			2500	2900	
0330/32	Molly Bear	36	40	41	41	45	45	48	58	95	95	95	105
0330/45	Molly Bear	84	97	100	100	100	100	105	125	160		175	193
0330/70	Molly Bear	190	250	265	265	265						410	451
0331/22	Molly Koala	37	40									76	84
0331/33	Molly Bear, Sitting									185	185	185	200
0331/40	Molly Koala	68	68									125	138
0332/33	Molly Dog										175	175	189
0332/45	Molly Petsy		95	98	98	98						180	194
0333/33	Molly Elephant, Sitting									185	185	185	200
0333/35	Molly Grizzly		95	98	98							180	194
0333/55	Molly Grizzly		170	175								330	356
0334/33	Molly Cat										175	175	189
0334/45	Molly Polar Bear		95	98	98							180	194
0334/55	Molly Polar Bear		140	145								270	292
0335/55	Molly Donkey		95	98	98	98	98	105	125	175		180	194
0335/80	Molly Donkey	185	250									370	407
0336/55	Molly Pony		95	98								198	214
0337/50	Schnauzer	138	170									270	297
0338/34	Molly Rabbit		69	70	70	70						125	133
0338/35	Molly Chow	63	76									115	127
0338/60	Molly Chow	145	175									230	253
0340/35	Molly Husky	72	89									115	127
0340/60	Molly Husky	145	175									230	253
0341/40	Super Molly Bear			90	90	90	95	125	170	170	170	187	
0341/65	Super Molly Bear			185	185	185	195	250	350	350	350	385	
0341/90	Super Molly Bear			300	300	300	320	400	600	600	600	660	

Numerical Listing

Steiff #	Description	80-81	81-82	82-83	83-84	84-85	85-86	86	87	88	89	90	Current
0341/98	Super Molly Bear				450	450	450	475	575			785	864
0341/99	Super Molly Bear	600	680	700	700							920	1012
0342/40	S-Molly St. Bernard					80	80					130	140
0342/60	S-Molly St. Bernard					150	150					245	265
0342/80	S-Molly St. Bernard					275	275	295				450	486
0342/98	S-Molly St. Bernard					400	400	425				660	713
0342/99	Super Molly Dog		680	700	700							1050	1134
0343/25	Molly Bear										150	97	105
0343/32	Molly Bear										220	145	157
0343/40	Molly Bear										325	205	221
0343/50	Molly Bello Dog							185	185			185	200
0343/80	Super Molly Seal	225	270	275	275							390	429
0344/99	S Molly Elephant					600	600	650				900	972
0345/25	Molly Woodchuck		43	43	43	43						80	86
0345/35	Molly Bear										205	135	146
0345/45	Molly Bear										290	185	200
0345/50	Molly Lynx	140	175									230	253
0345/60	Molly Bear										350	230	248
0345/80	Molly Bear										575	375	405
0346/30	Molly Groundhog	48	57	58	58	58	58	61	75	115		120	132
0347/55	Fox		148	150	150	150	150	160	195			280	302
0347/55	Molly Bear, Brown											165	178
0348/22	Molly Raccoon	42	52	53								110	121
0350/45	Molly Dog		95	98	98	98						180	194
0350/65	Molly Dog		157	160	160							295	319
0355/35	Molly Polar Bear, Sitting											135	146
0360/45	Molly Pig		95	98	98	98	98	105	125	175		180	194
0361/90	Super Molly Pig				275	275	275	295	375	525	525	310	341
0363/40	Molly Zicky Goat											115	124
0363/50	Molly Zicky Goat											150	162
0365/40	Molly Pony, Brown									125	125	77	83
0365/50	Molly Pony								175	235		235	254
0365/99	Super Molly Cow				400	400	400					700	770
0366/99	Super Molly Pony				400	400	400	425				700	770
0367/40	Molly Pony, Black									125		125	135
0367/99	Super Molly Donkey				400	400	400	425	425			700	770
0368/45	Molly Baby Lion										195	125	135
0370/30	Molly Leo Lion							70	85	125	135	87	94
0370/40	Molly Lamb		74	76	76	76						140	151
0370/70	Molly Leo Lion								295	400	400	250	270
0371/30	Molly Baby Lion											110	119
0375/45	Lion		175	180	180	180	180	195				342	369
0376/45	Molly Young Tiger										195	125	135
0376/60	Molly Young Tiger										330	330	356
0378/60	Molly Tiger									230	230	230	248
0380/28	Baloo Bear	46	51									225	248
0380/30	Molly Tiger Taky							70	85	125	135	87	94
0381/25	Bagheera Panther	48	53	53								225	248
0381/50	Super Molly Lion, Standing								280	380	380	380	410
0382/22	Baby Hathi Elephant	43	48									225	248
0382/60	Super Molly Lion, Lying								260	360	360	360	389
0383/22	King Louis Chimp	48	53	53								225	248
0385/75	Molly Puma					130	130			250		250	280
0385/98	Molly Puma						295					445	465
0387/75	Molly Panther					130	130	140	170	250	250	250	280
0387/98	Molly Panther						295	310				445	465
0390/40	Molly Leopard									160	160	105	113
0390/50	Molly Leopard							175		235	235	235	254
0405/40	Molly Camel									230	230	125	135
0405/60	Molly Camel									315	315	315	340
0409/19	Bear, Standing St 69"	2493	2593									4700	4800
0410/50	Bear on Wheels	200										685	754
0411/40	Molly Zebra									125	125	125	135
0417/60	Brown Bear Cub		175	180	180							340	367
0420/40	Molly Moose										230	145	157
0438/70	Super Molly Panda					195	205	250				320	346
0438/98	Super Molly Panda					425	450	450				695	751
0439/07	Panda				150								
0439/13	Panda				425								

Steiff #	Description	80-81	81-82	82-83	83-84	84-85	85-86	86	87	88	89	90	Current
0440/99	Goat									3550	3000	3300	
0445/60	Little Goat									1000	575	633	
0446/60	Little Goat									1000	575	633	
0450/99	Donkey									3975	3995	4395	
0453/75	Little Donkey									2750	2000	2200	
0460/45	Molly Husky									195	125	135	
0460/60	Molly Husky									330	330	356	
0467/23	Polar Bear, White	50	57	58							95	105	
0468/60	Polar Bear Cub		175	180	180						340	367	
0470/99	Polar Bear			2565	2565						4600	4700	
0472/99	Polar Bear			945	945	945	945	1195		1843	1700	1800	
0477/60	Panda Bear Cub		188	195	195						345	373	
0500/30	Bamboo Monkey, Light Brown							80	110		110	119	
0500/45	Bamboo Monkey, Light Brown							110	150		150	162	
0500/55	Bamboo Monkey, Light Brown							175	240		240	259	
0505/18	Elephant	38	42	43	43						75	83	
0505/30	Bamboo Monkey, Cream							80	110		110	119	
0505/45	Bamboo Monkey, Cream							110	150		150	162	
0505/55	Bamboo Monkey, Cream							175	240		240	259	
0520/50	Bongo Orang., Rust							185	250	250	250	270	
0525/50	Bongo Orang., Cream							185	250	250	250	270	
0535/32	Baby Gorilla										81	87	
0540/45	Gora Gorilla							185	250	250	150	162	
0540/60	Gora Gorilla							250	330	330	185	200	
0544/99	Gora Gorilla									1800	2000	2200	
0595/35	Mammouth, Trampy										105	113	
0609/16	Camel, Standing St 63"	2385	2495	2700	2778	2778			3334		4315	3895	4000
0710/35	Kangaroo/Baby	45	50	53	57	57	57	60			85	94	
0755/28	Giraffe	30	39	39	39	45	45	48			60	66	
0755/40	Giraffe	42	50	51	52	56	56	59			80	88	
0755/60	Giraffe	70	89	90	90	90	90				135	149	
0759/15	Giraffe St 60", mhr	1377	1450	1557	1557	1557	1557		1945		2593	2350	2400
0759/24	Giraffe St 96", mhr	2340	2500	2655	2655	2655	2655		3334		4769	4350	4600
0800/20	Lion	38	42								75	83	
0805/18	Lion, Standing	28									54	59	
0805/26	Lion, Standing	39	48								75	83	
0805/99	Lion, Standing									5694	6000	6500	
0807/99	Lioness, Lying									3750	4000	4500	
0809/11	Lion, Standing St 42"	2223	2547	2547	2547	2547	2547		2621		4300	4400	
0812/16	Rango Lion	38	43	43	43						75	83	
0815/15	Sulla Lioness	35	39	40							70	77	
0820/16	Wittie Tiger	35	39	40	40						70	77	
0822/99	Tiger, Standing St 59"	1800	2000	2210	2210	2210	2210		2778		3975	4100	
0825/16	Sigi Leopard	35	39	40	40						70	77	
0870/60	Tiger Cub "Pascha"					155	155	165	200	265	265	265	286
0885/50	Leopard, Lying			105	105	105	105				195	211	
0890/40	Leopard Cub	140	160	165	165						295	325	
0892/40	Kango Kangaroo with Baby									210	140	151	
1150/45	Seal Robby										96	104	
1170/16	Walrus									65	65	42	45
1172/80	Walrus									375	375	375	405
1172/99	Walrus									1600	1600	1600	1728
1174/55	Walrus									215		215	232
1175/14	Seal	31	35	36	36	36	36				60	66	
1175/20	Seal	49	59	60							95	105	
1178/14	Seal	31	38	38	38	38	38				60	66	
1179/04	Sealion Cub	125	140	145							235	259	
1210/25	Bear, Standing										81	87	
1212/25	Bear, Sitting										89	96	
1215/25	Bear, Lying										89	96	
1220/25	Polar Bear, Standing										81	87	
1222/25	Polar Bear, Sitting										89	96	
1225/25	Polar Bear, Lying										89	96	
1305/09	"Jumbo" Elephant, Mini-Mohair									50	50	54	
1305/12	"Jumbo" Elephant, Mini-Mohair									70	70	76	
1306/12	Waldi Hound, Tan, mhr										70	76	
1307/12	Kitty Cat, White, mhr										70	76	
1308/12	Mouse Fiep, Grey, mhr										60	65	
1310/12	Mouse Fiep, White, mhr										60	65	

Steiff #	Description	80-81	81-82	82-83	83-84	84-85	85-86	86	87	88	89	90	Current
1311/12	Fox Fuzzy, mhr											70	76
1312/12	Possy Squirrel, mhr											70	76
1313/12	Hound Waldi, Brown, mhr											70	76
1314/12	Cat Kitty, Black, mhr											70	76
1350/10	Timmy Rabbit, Mini-Mohair										50	50	54
1350/12	Timmy Rabbit, Mini-Mohair										70	70	76
1444/12	Browny Bear						23	24	30	50	50	32	35
1445/12	Browny Bear	17	20	21	23	29						42	46
1446/11	Koala Bear		22	23	23	23	23	25	30	42	42	45	49
1447/17	Polar Bear		25	26	26							50	54
1448/13	Kango Kangaroo										50	50	54
1450/12	Jumbo Elephant	17	20	21	23	29						39	43
1451/09	Rhino	16	18	19	19							39	43
1451/12	Jumbo Elephant						23	24	30	50	50	32	35
1453/14	Hockey Dromedary	17	20	21	23							39	43
1453/15	Trampy Camel						23	24	30	50		50	54
1456/09	Nosy Rhino						23	24	30	50		50	54
1457/14	Elk	25	28	28								60	66
1458/12	Bison	22	24	25								50	55
1460/13	Lion	17	20	21	23	31						39	43
1461/12	Leo Lion						23	24	30	50	50	32	35
1463/18	Gaty Crocodile						27	29	35	55	55	55	59
1464/12	Fox Woodland Animal							25	34	50		50	54
1465/10	Fox	19	21	22	22	24	24	26	32			45	50
1466/12	Squirrel Woodland Animal							25	36	50	50	32	35
1467/10	Squirrel	17	19	20	20	20	20					39	43
1468/10	Wild Boar	19	21	21	21	21	21	22	27	40		39	43
1470/12	Paddy Beaver		20	21	21	21	21	22	27	40	40	40	43
1472/07	Dolphin	11	14	14	14	14	14	15	18	30	30	30	33
1473/09	Seal	13	16	17	18	18	18	19	23	40	40	40	44
1474/10	Walrus	16	17	18	18	18						39	43
1476/12	Marmot Woodland Animal							25	34	50	50	50	54
1480/12	Ermine Woodland Animal							25	34			50	54
1493/13	Susi Cat, Grey			23	23	23	23	25	30	45		45	49
1493/14	Cat, Black			23	23	23						45	49
1495/10	Kitty Cat	14	16	17								39	43
1496/10	Black Tom Cat	22	24	25	25	25						52	57
1500/09	Hoppy, Lying, Brown	14	17	18	18							32	35
1500/13	Hoppy, Beige					25	25	27	33			35	38
1501/09	Hoppy, Lying, Grey	14	17	18	18							32	35
1501/13	Hoppy, Grey					25	25	27	33			35	38
1502/10	Manni, Sitting, Brown	14	17									32	35
1502/15	Manni, Beige					25	25	27	33			35	38
1503/10	Manni, Sitting, Grey	14	17									45	49
1503/15	Manni, Grey					25	25	27	33			35	38
1505/10	Piggy Pig		22	23	23	23	23	25	30	45	45	30	33
1510/14	Donkey	17	19	21	23	29	29					45	49
1512/16	Ossi, Zebra			25	26	26	26					48	52
1516/14	Pony	17	20	21	23	17	17	29				34	37
1518/11	Lamb	13	16	17	17	17	17	18	22			40	44
1520/11	Sheep, B/W	13	16	17	17	17	17	18	22			40	44
1522/14	Horse								38	58	58	37	40
1523/20	Shepherd and His Flock	69	80									320	352
1524/12	Cow								38	58	58	58	62
1525/08	Pig								34	50	50	50	54
1526/11	Dog	13	15									34	37
1526/12	Brown Baby Goat							36		50	55	55	59
1527/12	White Baby Lamb							36		50	55	55	59
1528/11	Fox Terrier	15	18	19	19	27	27					36	40
1530/12	Schnauzer	17	19									40	44
1532/12	Poodle, Black	18	20	21	21	21						40	44
1533/12	Poodle, White	18	20	21	21	21						40	44
1540/20	Xorry Fox, Lying							40	48	70	70	46	50
1542/35	Red Fox, Sleeping	67	75	76	76	76	76	80	96	120	120	74	85
1543/35	Raccoon, Sleeping	67	67									175	188
1544/35	Fox, Sleeping, Beige	70	78	79	79							175	195
1548/25	Fuzzy Fox										115	78	84
1550/12	Owl Woodland Animal							25	30	50	50	31	33
1670/06	Hedgehog, Lying, mhr	4	5	5	6	6	6	7	8	14	14	14	15

Numerical Listing

Steiff #	Description	80-81	81-82	82-83	83-84	84-85	85-86	86	87	88	89	90	Current
1670/10	Hedgehog, Lying, mhr	9	10	13	14	16	16					44	48
1670/17	Hedgehog, Lying, mhr	17	21	23	25	28	28					75	83
1675/12	Joggi Hedgehog						18	19	23	40	40	25	27
1675/18	Joggi Hedgehog						24	25	30	50	50	50	54
1675/35	Hedgehog Joggi											93	100
1675/45	Super Joggi Hedgehog							60	145	220		220	238
1675/70	Super Joggi Hedgehog							295	360	500		500	540
1677/14	Joggi Hedgehog, Begging						24	25	30	50	50	32	35
1677/20	Hedgehog Joggi											46	50
1677/50	Hedgehog									350		350	378
1680/12	Hedgehog, Begging, mhr	16	20	21	22	22	22					70	77
1820/14	Fawn	24	26	27	27							58	64
1830/40	Deer, Standing	85	95	98								155	171
1831/20	Fawn, Lying									75	75	48	52
1831/38	Fawn, Lying	55	63	64	64	64	64	68	82	100	100	100	109
1834/40	Lamb	66										120	132
1835/22	Fawn, Standing									100	100	100	107
1837/30	Doe, Lying									120	120	120	130
1838/30	Roebuck, Standing									145	145	145	157
1840/26	Diggy Badger							60	72	110		115	124
1840/36	Diggy Badger							80	100	150		165	178
2015/24	Squirrel								135		135	86	93
2025/18	Chipmunk Chippy										90	60	65
2030/20	Squirrel	31	37	38						75		58	64
2032/25	Possy Squirrel			41	41	41	41	44				75	81
2040/12	Perri Squirrel, mhr	18	22	23	23							85	94
2040/17	Perri Squirrel, mhr	22										110	121
2040/25	Putsi Otter, Standing							85	110			115	124
2042/24	Marmot Piff, Grey/Brown											63	68
2045/25	Putsi Otter, Sitting							85	110			115	124
2050/25	Raggy Racoon, Standing							95	125	125		81	87
2055/35	Raggy Racoon, Sitting							145	195	195		120	130
2060/20	Raggy Ringel Racoon							65	90	90		57	62
2070/25	Piff Marmot, Standing							85	110	110		110	119
2080/35	Skunk									160		105	113
2121/18	Beaver	29										55	61
2125/20	Nagy Beaver		34	35	35	35	35	37	37			65	70
2150/12	Goldy Hamster						24	25	30	50		50	54
2150/16	Goldy Hamster						29	31	38	62		65	70
2150/50	Super Goldy Hamster						295	310	310	310		310	335
2155/12	Hamster	17	20	21	21	21						34	37
2155/17	Hamster	22	27	27	27	27						42	46
2160/20	"Otty" Otter			30								55	59
2170/10	Mouse, White	11	13	14	14	14	14	15	18	30	30	30	33
2171/10	Mouse, Grey	11	13	14	14	14	14	15	18	30	30	30	33
2180/12	Mole/Shovel, mhr	11	14	18	19	19	19	20	24	40		45	55
2180/15	Maxi Mole	22	29	30	30	30	30					45	50
2205/12	Woodchuck	24	26	27	27	27	27					49	54
2251/18	Guinea Pig Ginny											37	40
2251/22	Guinea Pig Ginny											44	48
2252/10	Guinea Pig	19	21	22	22	22	22	23	28	40		42	46
2254/15	Guinea Pig				29	29		31				48	52
2255/15	Guinea Pig, Mama	24	30									49	54
2256/15	Guinea Pig, Papa	24	30	31	31							48	53
2270/22	Mouse Pieps, Grey											66	71
2270/25	Otter	32	32									65	72
2270/35	Otter	54										95	105
2275/22	Mouse Pieps, White											66	71
2300/10	Fish, Blue, mhr	8	9									40	47
2301/10	Fish, Gold, mhr	8	9									40	47
2311/25	Fish, Green	28										52	55
2320/25	Dolphin	23	26	27	27							44	46
2320/35	Dolphin	28	33	33	33							55	58
2322/35	Finny Dolphin								57	75		75	81
2322/50	Finny Dolphin								89	120		120	130
2322/99	Finny Dolphin								450	600		600	648
2370/08	Frog, Sitting	17	20	21	21	24	24	26	32			39	41
2380/32	Frog, Dangling	29	32	32	32	32						57	60
2455/14	Turtle	19	23	24	24	24						85	89

Steiff #	Description	80-81	81-82	82-83	83-84	84-85	85-86	86	87	88	89	90	Current
2455/22	Turtle	36										135	142
2460/30	Ladybug/Wheels, mhr	145										445	450
2505/12	Penguin	16	19	19	20	20	20	21	26	37	37	37	41
2505/27	Penguin	35	40	41								70	77
2505/40	Penguin	59	77									115	127
2507/20	Baby Penguin				33	33	33	35	42	70	70	70	76
2507/38	Penguin			72	72	72	72	76	92	135		130	140
2509/09	Penguin St 36"	450	450	450	450	450	450		620		834	850	875
2510/40	Charly Penguin								115	150	150	150	162
2511/26	Paddy Puffin	57	65									115	127
2531/13	Parakeet, Gold/Green	18	22	23	23	23	23					54	59
2534/13	Parakeet, White/Blue	18	22	23	23	23	23	25	30	47	47	47	52
2540/30	Parrot, Red, Studio	76	89	90	90	90	90		130			225	265
2541/30	Parrot, Blue, Studio	76	89	90	90	90	90		130			225	265
2544/30	Lora Parrot, Red								95	125		125	135
2545/30	Cockatoo			90	90	90						180	194
2550/30	Lora Parrot, Green								95	125		165	178
2555/14	Parrot Lori											45	49
2560/14	Tucan Tucky											45	49
2560/20	Tucky Tucan										105	105	113
2565/14	Pelican Peli											45	49
2565/20	Peli Pelican										105	105	113
2570/14	Penguin Peggy											45	49
2580/14	Raven Hucky											45	49
2590/50	Owl		295									475	513
2591/22	Owlet		50	50	50	50	50	53	65	90	90	90	97
2592/25	Baby Owl "Wiggy"											59	64
2593/28	Screech Owl		97	99	99	99	99	105	125	190		195	211
2603/28	Woodpecker, Spotted	82	82									158	165
2604/28	Woodpecker, Green	82	82									158	165
2605/20	Kingfisher 8"	82	82									158	165
2606/50	Heron 20"	190	190	195	195	195						360	365
2608/50	Stork 20"	200	200	200	200	200						380	395
2612/20	Swan, White				40	40	40					75	81
2615/28	Falcon, Studio	85	97	99	99	99	99	105	125	195		200	220
2620/99	Peacock, Studio	800	950	1000	1000	1000	1000		1400	1600	1963	1700	2000
2621/80	Peacock, Studio	750	900	900	1000							1500	1600
2622/18	Wittie Eagle Owl								55	75	75	75	81
2622/24	Wittie Eagle Owl								89	120		120	130
2622/40	Pheasant	260	295	295	295							495	500
2623/40	Golden Pheasant	275	300	315	315							550	600
2625/15	Owl	26	30	31	31	31	31	33	40			58	63
2625/25	Owl	41	50	50	50							80	88
2650/23	Young Wild Boar									120		120	130
2655/28	Young Wild Boar "Wutzi"											100	105
2655/40	Young Wild Boar "Wutzi"											135	143
2660/20	Bora Wild Boar								57	75		75	81
2660/30	Bora Wild Boar								89	120		120	130
2675/15	Wild Boar	33	39	39	39	39	39					65	72
2675/20	Wild Boar			50	52	65	65					90	97
2677/30	Baby Boar			81	81	81	81	86				140	151
2678/50	Wild Boar St		230	235	235	235						425	459
2690/32	Scottish Highland Bull									180	180	180	194
2695/35	Buffalo									200	200	200	216
2710/28	Cat Minka, Standing											92	98
2715/35	Cat Minka, Lying											84	89
2720/22	Cat, Grey	37	37									70	77
2725/22	Cat, Spotted	37	45									70	77
2726/17	Sissi Cat	35	38	39	39	39	39	41	50	75	75	47	52
2726/22	Sissi Cat	45	49	50	50	50	50	53	65	95		95	105
2728/17	Lizzy Cat	35	38	39	39	39	39	41	50	75	75	75	83
2728/22	Lizzy Cat	45	49	50	50	50	50	53	65	95		95	105
2732/17	Tabby	35	38	39	39							75	83
2735/16	Sulla Cat, Cream					38	38	40				75	81
2735/26	Sulla Cat, Cream					58	58	61				105	113
2736/16	Sulla Cat, Grey					38	38	40	48	75		75	81
2736/26	Sulla Cat, Grey					58	58	61	75	105		105	113
2738/16	Dossy Cat, Black					38	38	40	48	75	75	75	81
2738/26	Dossy Cat, Black					58	58	61	75	105	105	105	113

Steiff #	Description	80-81	81-82	82-83	83-84	84-85	85-86	86	87	88	89	90	Current
2740/25	Siamese	57	63	64	64							120	132
2742/23	Cat									120	120	200	216
2745/30	Cat, Lying			75	75							130	140
2750/22	Ringel Cat, Lying		50	50	50							90	97
2752/26	Persian Cat, Grey			62	63	63	63					110	119
2752/35	Persian Cat, Grey			110	110	110						195	211
2753/26	Angora Cat, White			62	63	63	63					110	119
2754/25	Minou Cat, Lying, Cream							70	85	120	120	120	130
2754/40	Minou Cat, Lying, Cream							100	125	175	175	120	130
2755/25	Minou Cat, Lying, Grey							70	85	120		120	130
2755/40	Minou Cat, Lying, Grey							100	125	175		175	189
2756/25	Minou Cat, Lying, Black							70	85	120	120	120	130
2756/40	Minou Cat, Lying, Black							100	125	175		175	189
2757/25	Minou Cat, Striped								92	120	120	120	130
2757/40	Minou Cat, Striped								130	175	175	175	189
2758/40	Cat									175	175	175	189
2877/30	Jr. Petsy			74	74	74						130	140
2881/35	Fox, Crouching	70	85									140	154
2882/25	Jr. Rabbit, Lying	38	38									75	83
2882/35	Jr. Fox Terrier			81	89	89	89	95				165	178
2882/35	Jr. Rabbit, Lying	57	57									110	121
2883/30	Jr. Schnauzer, Sitting	67										120	132
2883/35	Jr. Charly Dog			81	81	81	81	86				140	151
2884/26	Jr. Cockie		75	75	75							125	135
2884/30	Jr. Schnauzer, Lying	67										120	132
2885/28	Dog, Sitting	59	70									110	121
2886/28	Dog, Lying	59	70									110	121
2887/26	Swiss Mtn Dog			75	75							140	151
2888/35	St. Bernard	90	110	115	115							170	187
2890/22	Jr. Pekinese			53	53	53	53					95	103
2892/28	Jr. Fuzzy Fox		79	80	80							150	162
2893/30	Jr. Scotch Terrier			74	74	74						135	146
2897/30	Jr. Leo Lion Cub			91	95	95	95	100	100	180	180	180	194
2910/12	Snuffy Rabbit, Brown	15	19	19								32	35
2910/18	Snuffy Rabbit, Brown	19	24	24								38	42
2911/12	Snuffy Rabbit, Grey	15	19	19								32	35
2911/18	Snuffy Rabbit, Grey	19	24	24								38	42
2912/18	Snuffy Elephant							50	65			65	70
2914/18	Snuffy Lion							55	75	75		75	81
2916/16	Snuffy Fox							50	67	67		67	72
2918/18	Snuffy Pig							50	66	66		66	71
2920/16	Snuffy Bear			29	29	29	31	38				50	54
2921/16	Snuffy Bear								42	56		60	65
2923/16	Snuffy Dog			32	32	32	34	42	62			62	67
2926/16	Snuffy Cat			32	32	32						55	59
2927/16	Snuffy Cat			32	32	32						55	59
2928/16	Snuffy Cat							50	65	65		42	45
2931/16	Snuffy, Beige/White			29	29	29	30	38	55			55	59
2932/16	Snuffy, Caramel			29	29	29	30	38	55			55	59
2933/16	Snuffy, Dark Brown			29	29	29	30	38	55			55	59
2945/25	Rabbit	37	47	48								70	77
2947/35	Ossi, Standing	38	42									70	77
2950/32	Mummy Rabbit, Begging, Beige									120	125	125	135
2955/18	Winni, Grey, Sitting	30	33									60	66
2955/32	Mummy Rabbit, Begging, Grey									120	125	125	135
2956/16	Hoppel Rabbit											37	39
2956/18	Winni, Brown, Sitting	30	33									60	66
2957/13	Hoppel, Grey	33	37	37	37							62	68
2957/22	Hoppel Rabbit											63	67
2958/13	Poppel, Beige	33	37	37	37							62	68
2958/25	Hoppel Rabbit											63	67
2960/22	Sonny, Grey	45	50	51	51	51	51	54	65			86	93
2961/22	Ronny, Beige	45	50	51	51	51	51	54	65			86	93
2962/16	Mummy, Grey	32	35	36	36							61	66
2962/25	Poppel Rabbit											63	67
2963/16	Pummy, Beige	32	35	36	36							60	66
2965/20	Rabbit, Sitting	29	35	35								46	51
2965/25	Rabbit, Sitting	38	50									70	77
2968/35	Snobby Rabbit				72	72	72	76	95			120	130

Numerical Listing

Steiff #	Description	80-81	81-82	82-83	83-84	84-85	85-86	86	87	88	89	90	Current
2970/23	B/W, Spotted	43	51	52	52	52						85	92
2970/30	B/W, Spotted	72	89	90	90							150	162
2972/40	Dormy Rabbit, Lying									165	175	110	119
2974/16	Dormili Rabbit							35	50	73	75	47	51
2975/25	Dormy Rabbit						67	71	86	120	125	75	81
2977/20	Dormili Rabbit							37	50	75		75	81
2978/35	Dormy Rabbit, Begging								115	160	165	165	178
2982/17	B/W Spottili, Running							55		75	80	80	86
2984/17	B/W Spottili, Sitting							53		73	75	75	81
2985/30	B/W Spotty, Sitting							100		140		140	151
2992/17	Grey & White Spottili, Running							55		75	80	80	86
2994/17	Grey & White Spottili, Sitting							53		73	75	75	81
2995/30	Grey & White Spotty, Sitting							100		140	150	150	162
3020/00	Manni Rabbit Set, 3 pc., 1983, LE					175	175					375	413
3020/10	Manni Rabbit, mhr			35								95	110
3020/30	Manni Rabbit, mhr			75	75	75						175	195
3135/45	Ango	53	65	65								100	110
3141/43	Lulac, Brown, mhr	36	44									135	155
3142/43	Lulac, Grey, mhr	36										135	155
3155/16	Timmy, Brown	23	28	28	28							45	49
3156/16	Timmy, Grey	23	28	28	28							45	49
3205/15	Tulla Duck	23	27	28	28	28	28	30	36			43	47
3210/16	Willa Duck, Green									46	48	48	52
3210/22	Willa Duck, Green									60		60	65
3211/16	Pilla Duck, Blue									46		50	54
3211/22	Pilla Duck, Blue									60		60	65
3215/16	Tulla Duck, Red									46		50	54
3215/22	Tulla Duck, Red									60		60	65
3230/11	Duck Daggi										35	35	38
3232/11	Duck Daggi										35	35	38
3240/16	Duck Waggi											35	37
3240/20	Duck Waggi											48	51
3242/08	Piccy Duck	10	11	11								25	38
3242/11	Piccy Duck	14	16	16								32	35
3243/16	Duck Waggi											35	37
3243/20	Duck Waggi											48	51
3247/26	Swan	57	65	66								140	154
3450/22	Locky Lamb	36	40									72	79
3455/17	Zicky Goat			38	38	38						70	76
3455/23	Zicky Goat			60	60							100	108
3460/20	Rocky Wild Goat			41	43	43						80	86
3460/25	Lamb Lamby										77	77	83
3460/30	Lamb Lamby										95	95	103
3462/22	Lamb Lamby										65	43	46
3464/22	Lamb Lamby, Brown										65	43	46
3475/40	Elbow Puppet-Leopard	74	80	82								140	168
3476/40	Elbow Puppet-Skunk	80	87	88								150	180
3477/50	Elbow Puppet-Raccoon	80	87	88								150	180
3478/50	Elbow Puppet-Puma/Lion	86	94									170	204
3480/40	Elbow Puppet-Rabbit, Grey	58	60	61	65	65	65	69	69			100	120
3480/41	Rabbit, White							69	69			115	124
3481/40	Elbow Puppet-Rabbit, Brown	58	60	61	65	65	65	69				110	132
3483/40	Elbow Puppet-Cat	70	76									135	162
3490/45	Mimic Bear				75	75	75	79	95			165	178
3492/45	Mimic Dog				75	75	75	79	95			120	130
3515/14	Snuffy Fox	19	24									38	42
3515/18	Snuffy Fox	25	32									50	55
3518/14	Snuffy Lion	19	24	24								38	42
3518/18	Snuffy Lion	25	32	32								50	55
3520/12	Snuffy Cat, Beige	17	21	22								36	40
3520/17	Snuffy Cat, Beige	22	28									40	44
3521/12	Snuffy Cat, Grey	17	21	22								36	40
3521/17	Snuffy Cat, Grey	22	28	29								40	44
3605/20	Donkey	29	36	37								56	62
3605/27	Donkey	39	47									75	83
3710/60	Pony on Wheels	225										675	695
3750/18	Pony, Brown, mhr	24	29									120	125
3760/25	Horse, Brown	57	63	64	65	65	65					110	119
3785/25	Horse, Beige	53	58	59	59							100	110

Numerical Listing

Steiff #	Description	80-81	81-82	82-83	83-84	84-85	85-86	86	87	88	89	90	Current
3790/18	Calf	34	38	38								65	72
3792/25	Cow	57	63	64	64							110	121
3795/27	Calf, Lying			66	72	72	72	76	93			115	124
3810/17	Pig	34	38	38	38	38	38	40	48	70	70	45	55
4003	Goldilocks 16" & Three Steiff Bears, Reeves International, (0173/25, Boy; 0173/30, Mother; 0173/32, Father)												300
4004	Goldilocks 8" & Three Steiff Bears, Reeves International, (0173/25, Boy; 0173/18, Mother; 0173/22 Father),												200
4005	Alice, (13cm Steiff Cat; 13cm Steiff Mouse; 20cm Rabbit with big pocket watch), LE 3000												250
4010/12	Mopsy Dog, mhr	17	20									75	79
4026/21	Spaniel "Cockie", Sitting											74	80
4028/32	Spaniel "Cockie", Lying											88	95
4030/14	Pekinese		40	41	41	43	43					75	81
4035/38	Cocker Spaniel					80	80	85	110	150		150	162
4040/99	St. Bernard Dog	450	615	610	665							1065	1200
4045/35	Boxer				80	80	80	85	105	175	175	175	189
4045/50	Boxer, Lying			130	130	130	130	138	165	250	250	105	113
4048/40	German Shepherd				80	80	80					135	146
4048/50	German Shepherd			130	130	130	130	138	165	250		250	270
4050/80	Shepherd, Standing	665	775	796	796							1200	1320
4052/80	Shepherd, Lying	565	625	639	639							1075	1182
4053/20	German Shepherd Puppy				33	33	33					55	59
4053/23	Shepherd, Puppy	66	74	75	75	75	75					125	138
4055/65	Husky	580	650									995	1095
4060/80	Setter, Standing	520	600									1000	1100
4061/80	Setter, Sitting	520	600	602	602							1100	1210
4065/65	Chow	545	600	602	602	585						1000	1100
4070/55	Schnauzer	245	275	285	285							490	539
4075/60	Boxer	500	575	575	745	745						1110	1221
4080/50	Terrier	255	285	285	285	285						490	539
4085/28	Terrier	72	79									135	149
4090/40	Collie				80	80	80	85	110			160	173
4121/30	Pomeranian, White	72	80	82	82							135	149
4122/30	Pomeranian, Rust	72	80									135	149
4130/20	"Mobby" Bobtail Dog, Sitting									80	80	80	86
4132/24	"Mobby" Bobtail Dog, Standing									125	125	125	135
4140/30	Fox Terrier "Treff"									145	145	92	98
4142/12	Dachshund	24	26	27	27	30	30	32				45	50
4150/25	Raudi Dachshund, Sand/Grey							75	90	135		135	146
4150/40	Raudi Dachshund, Sand/Grey							100	125	190		190	205
4151/25	Raudi Dachshund, Grey/Brown							75	90	135		135	146
4151/40	Raudi Dachshund, Grey/Brown							100	125	190		190	205
4153/25	Dog Raudi											98	104
4156/26	Poodle, Brown	55	60									105	116
4157/26	Poodle, Black	55	60									105	116
4157/50	Poodle, Standing	255	285	285	285							495	545
4158/50	Poodle, Upright	275	300									540	594
4160/24	Welfo Puppy, Standing							95	125	125		125	135
4160/35	Poodle, Black	67	74									120	132
4161/35	Poodle, White	67	74									120	132
4162/22	Welfo Puppy, Lying							100	135			140	151
4162/35	Poodle, Apricot	67	74									120	132
4165/45	Wolfi Dog, Lying								225	300		320	346
4167/40	Shepherd Dog "Arco", Sitting											135	143
4168/45	Shepherd Dog Arco, Lying											170	180
4180/45	Afgan Dog, Standing								235	315		325	351
4182/40	Afgan Dog, Sitting								175	230		245	260
4184/35	Blacky S. Terrier										160	160	173
4185/35	Whity W.H. Terrier										160	160	173
4192/25	Yorkshire Terrier, Sitting								125	165	165	165	178
4215/21	Fox Terrier	48	52									85	94
4215/30	Fox Terrier	73										135	149
4900/22	Fox	22										42	46
5030/17	Pummy Bear										90	90	97
5030/21	Pummy Bear										115	115	124
5035/17	Pummy Koala Bear										105	105	113

Steiff #	Description	80-81	81-82	82-83	83-84	84-85	85-86	86	87	88	89	90	Current
5035/21	Pummy Koala Bear										140	80	86
5060/17	Pummy Rabbit										95	60	65
5060/21	Pummy Rabbit										130	83	89
5063/17	Pummy Rabbit										95	95	103
5063/21	Pummy Rabbit										130	130	140
5067/17	Pummy Rabbit										95	95	103
5067/21	Pummy Rabbit										130	130	140
5250/17	Fox Pummy										100	66	71
5250/21	Fox Pummy										135	88	93
5322/35	Panther, Lying	58	75									110	121
5322/50	Panther, Lying	98										180	198
5340/33	Cosy Elephant, Lying									120		120	130
5350/15	Cosy Jumbo Elephant				39	39	41	52	70	70		70	76
5350/22	Cosy Jumbo Elephant				60	60	64	80		110		110	123
5350/30	Cosy Jumbo Elephant					100	100					165	178
5351/40	Leopard, Lying	76	84	85								140	154
5352/25	Cosy Elephant			58	58							95	103
5352/33	Cosy Bear									110		110	119
5353/25	Cosy Bear, Honey Gold			53	53							95	103
5354/25	Cosy Bear, Dk. Brown			53	53							65	70
5355/26	Cosy Bear		35	35	35	35	35	37	45			95	103
5355/36	Cosy Bear		55	55	55	55	55	58	70			95	103
5357/25	Cosy Panda				67	67	70	90	120			120	130
5358/18	Cosy Koala							45	55	80		80	86
5358/27	Cosy Koala			58	58	58	58					95	103
5358/28	Cosy Koala							70	85	125		125	135
5358/38	Cosy Koala							100	125			160	173
5358/50	Cosy Koala							200	250			320	346
5360/25	Cosy Pony			45	46	46	46					85	92
5360/40	Pony	76	83	85	85	85						135	149
5361/24	Cosy Manni			43	43	43						80	86
5362/24	Cosy Hoppy			43	43	43	43					80	86
5363/16	Cosy Snuffy, Beige			28	28	28	28	30	36			45	49
5364/16	Cosy Snuffy, Caramel			28	28	28	28		36			45	49
5368/33	Cosy Dog								95			95	103
5370/28	Cosy Panther	57	63	63	63	63	63	67	82	110		110	121
5372/33	Cosy Puma		64	65	65	65	65					120	130
5374/17	Cosy Seal					25	25	27	33	45		45	49
5374/35	Cosy Seal			49	49	49	49	52	63	90		90	97
5375/30	Cosy Seal "Robby", Grey							45	58	85		85	92
5375/31	Cosy Seal "Robby", Beige							45	58	85		85	92
5375/57	Cosy Seal			81	81	81	81					145	157
5376/11	Preppy Duck, Boy						20	21	28	40		40	43
5376/12	Preppy Duck, Girl						20	21	28	40		40	43
5376/50	Cosy Seal	125	126									230	248
5377/12	Cosy Piccy Duck			17	18	18	18					32	35
5378/17	Cosy Daggi Duck			21	22	22	22	23				39	42
5382/43	Cosy Froggy		70									135	146
5384/16	Cosy Froggy Frog							44	53	80	80	52	56
5384/20	Cosy Froggy Frog						44	47	57	57		57	62
5384/28	Cosy Froggy Frog						75	80	96	96		96	104
5384/50	Super Cosy Froggy Frog							325	395	395		445	481
5387/27	Cosy Whale				27	27	27	29	36	55		45	49
5390/30	Cosy Mouse, Blue		42									80	86
5391/30	Cosy Mouse, Violet		42									80	84
5392/15	Cosy Mouse, Olive		22										
5392/30	Cosy Mouse, Green		42	43	43	43	43					80	86
5393/15	Cosy Mouse, White		22	23	23	23	23					40	43
5393/45	Cosy Fiep Mouse, White								145	190		190	205
5394/15	Cosy Mouse, Grey		22	23	23							40	43
5394/45	Cosy Fiep Mouse, Grey								145	190		190	205
5396/17	Cosy Nagy Beaver							31	40	60	60	60	65
5396/22	Cosy Nagy Beaver							46	65	95		95	103
5397/15	Cosy Hedgehog	20	21	21	21	21						39	42
5397/25	Cosy Joggi Hedgehog	30	30	30	30							55	59
5405/17	Cosy Polar Bear					35	35	37	47	47		47	51
5405/30	Cosy Polar Bear				50	50	50	53	64	95	95	95	103
5410/80	Cosy Dolphin		157									250	270
5414/18	Cosy Piggy Pig						30	32	39	63	63	40	43

Steiff #	Description	80-81	81-82	82-83	83-84	84-85	85-86	86	87	88	89	90	Current
5415/28	Cosy Pig			49	52	52	52	55	66	100	95	61	66
5420/19	Cosy Nosy Rhino, Lying									95		95	103
5420/75	Cosy Nosy Rhino, Lying									300		300	324
5420/99	Cosy Nosy Rhino, Lying									1600		1600	1728
5422/20	Cosy Nosy Rhino, Standing									95		95	103
5422/40	Cosy Nosy Rhino, Standing									150		150	162
5432/20	Snail "Nelly", Purple									55		55	59
5434/20	Snail Nelly, Brown									55		55	59
5438/25	Dolphin "Finny", Ice Blue									53		53	57
5440/16	Cosy Sulla, Cream						40	43	52	52		52	56
5440/22	Cosy Sulla, Cream						50	53	65			65	70
5442/16	Cosy Milla, Blonde						40	43	52			52	56
5442/22	Cosy Milla, Blonde						50	53	65	65		65	70
5445/20	Cosy Poodle "Tobby", Stndg, Apricot							50	60	90		90	97
5445/28	Cosy Poodle "Tobby", Stndg, Apricot							70	87	135		135	146
5447/20	Cosy Poodle Tobby, Stndg, Black							50	60	90		90	97
5447/28	Cosy Poodle "Tobby", Stndg, Black							70	87	135		135	146
5450/27	Cosy Gora Monkey	79	80	80								145	157
5452/28	Cosy Poodle "Nobby", Lying, Grey							75	90	135		135	146
5457/20	Cosy Dog "Bello" Standing, Grey							50	60	90		90	97
5457/27	Cosy Bello-Dog				63	63						100	108
5460/35	Cosy Daschund		81	81	81	81						145	157
5463/50	Cosy Basset Dog			125	125	135	165			225		225	243
5465/16	Cosy Lumpi Schnauzer						34	36	44	70		70	76
5465/27	Cosy Lumpi Schnauzer						55	58	71	120		120	130
5466/16	Cosy Lumpi Schnauzer, Lying						36	38	46	75		75	81
5472/20	Cosy Grissy Donkey							44	53	80	80	80	86
5472/28	Cosy Grissy Donkey				66	66		70	87	87		87	94
5473/25	Cosy Lamby							52	71	110		110	119
5473/40	Cosy Lamby							72	115	175		175	189
5474/21	Cosy Lamb						39	41	50	70		70	76
5474/27	Cosy Lamb						60	65	78	115		115	124
5475/20	Cosy Horse "Ferdy", Brown							44	53	80	80	50	54
5475/28	Cosy Horse "Ferdy"					59		62	75	125	125	125	135
5476/20	Cosy Horse "Yello", Beige							44	53	80		80	86
5477/25	Cosy Flora Cow					59		62	75	125		125	135
5480/22	Cosy Zicky Goat								70	100		110	119
5491/18	Gocki Rooster								58	85	85	85	92
5495/18	Gacki Hen								58	85	85	85	92
5498/10	Cosy Bibi Chick							19	27			30	32
5502/13	Cosy Minni, Sitting, Beige/White									42	44	44	47
5503/13	Cosy Minni, Sitting, Brown/Cream									42	44	44	47
5504/13	Cosy Minni, Sitting, Grey/White									42	44	44	47
5505/13	Cosy Minni, Sitting, Black/White									42	44	44	47
5505/25	Cuddly Bear			50	50							95	103
5507/15	Manni, Begging, Brown/White									44	46	46	50
5508/15	Manni, Begging, Brown/Cream									44		44	48
5511/18	Cosy Snuffy, Crouching, Beige/White									60		60	65
5512/18	Cosy Snuffy, Crouching, Rust/Beige									60		60	65
5513/16	Cosy Bunny, Aubergine											37	39
5514/16	Cosy Bunny, Blackberry											37	39
5520/25	Cat, Grey		50	50	50	50						90	97
5525/25	Rabbit, Brown		50	50	50							92	99
5526/25	Ango, White	50	51	51	51							95	103
5530/25	Cuddly Dog		50	50								90	97
5558/10	Mini Cosy Hedgehog							15	18	28	28	28	30
5565/10	Blue Bird								19	30		32	35
5567/10	Brown Bird								19	30		32	35
5578/11	Penquin								23	30		32	35
5585/15	Blue Dolphin								23	35		35	38
5588/15	Grey Dolphin								23	35		35	38
5600/18	Floppy Bear			36	36	36		38	48	65		65	70
5600/25	Floppy Bear			50	50	50						95	103
5605/18	Floppy Rabbit			36	36	36		38	48	69		69	75
5605/25	Floppy Rabbit			50	50	50			50			85	92
5610/18	Floppy Dog			36	36	38		38	48	70		70	76
5610/25	Floppy Dog			50								85	92
5620/18	Floppy Cat			36	36	36		38	48	70		60	65
5620/25	Floppy Cat			50	50	50		53	65	100		100	107

Steiff #	Description	80-81	81-82	82-83	83-84	84-85	85-86	86	87	88	89	90	Current
5625/18	Floppy Lamb			36	36	36	38	48		65		70	76
5625/25	Floppy Lamb			50	50	50	53	65		95		95	103
5651/16	Mini Floppy Bear										50	50	54
5652/16	Min Floppy Polar Bear										50	50	54
5655/16	Mini Floppy Elephant										53	53	57
5658/16	Mini Floppy Rabbit										50	50	54
5662/16	Mini Floppy Dog										53	53	57
5665/16	Mini Floppy Cat										50	50	54
5668/16	Mini Floppy Lamb										50	50	54
5672/16	Mini Floppy Donkey										53	53	57
5675/16	Mini Floppy Pig										50	50	54
5678/16	Mini Floppy Fox										53	53	57
5700/20	Teddy	39	43	43								85	94
5700/30	Teddy	57	62	62								120	132
5701/22	Kiddi Bear										75	75	81
5702/20	Kiddi Bear										75	75	81
5706/20	Kiddi Elephant										75	75	81
5710/20	Elephant	45										80	88
5710/30	Elephant	61	66									110	121
5712/20	Kiddi Dog										75	75	81
5715/20	Cocki	41	44	45								75	83
5715/30	Cocki	59	65									110	121
5717/20	Kiddi Cat										75	75	81
5717/20	Terrier	41	44									75	83
5717/30	Terrier	59	65									100	110
5720/20	Cat	39	43									69	76
5720/30	Cat	57	62									100	110
5722/20	Kiddi Mouse										75	75	81
5725/20	Floppy Lamb			41								75	81
5725/20	Kiddi Hedgehog										75	75	81
5725/30	Floppy Lamb			59								110	119
5728/20	Kiddi Fox										75	75	81
5750/22	Drolly Bear											52	56
5780/22	Drolly Cat											52	55
5790/22	Drolly Fox											52	55
5810/22	Elephant	43	48	49	49	49						79	87
5820/22	Dog	43	48									79	87
6020/32	Poppy Raccoon										135	135	146
6060/24	Poppy Rabbit, Blond										80	80	86
6060/32	Poppy Rabbit, Blond										130	130	140
6062/24	Poppy Rabbit, Cinnamon										80	52	56
6062/32	Poppy Rabbit, Cinnamon										130	83	89
6067/24	Poppy Rabbit, Grey										80	80	86
6067/32	Poppy Rabbit, Grey										130	130	140
6080/32	Poppy Cat										135	135	146
6190/30	Chimp	38	47									75	83
6202/14	Friedericke, Yellow Goose									47	49	31	33
6203/26	Friedericke Yellow Goose, Drsd Grl									80	85	85	92
6205/14	Frederic, White Gander									47	49	31	33
6206/26	Frederic, White Gander									80	85	85	92
6210/20	Cuddly Goose, Yellow										65	65	70
6210/32	Cuddly Goose, Yellow										100	100	108
6212/20	Cuddly Goose, Brown										65	65	70
6212/32	Cuddly Goose, Brown										100	100	108
6212/50	Cuddly Goose, Brown										200	200	216
6215/28	Possy Guenon Monkey										120	120	130
6215/30	Fox	40										72	79
6220/28	Possy Elephant										125	125	135
6225/28	Possy Cat										115	115	125
6228/28	Possy Lion										120	120	130
6235/30	Rabbit	40	40									70	77
6235/40	Rabbit	54	54									92	101
6240/20	Toldi Chimp			25	28							46	50
6240/28	Possy Fox										120	78	84
6240/30	Toldi Chimp			49	53							90	97
6242/20	Toldi Bear			25	28							48	52
6242/30	Toldi Bear			49	53	53						90	97
6245/28	Possy Hedgehog										115	115	124
6270/27	Toldi Bear									80		80	86

Numerical Listing

Steiff #	Description	80-81	81-82	82-83	83-84	84-85	85-86	86	87	88	89	90	Current
6271/27	Toldi Elephant									85		85	92
6272/27	Toldi Monkey									80		80	86
6273/27	Toldi Hedgehog									80	80	80	86
6274/27	Toldi Frog									80		80	86
6275/27	Toldi Cat									90		90	97
6276/27	Toldi Dog									80		80	86
6280/40	Dangling Rabbit		52									90	97
6280/70	Dangling Monkey											240	254
6281/25	Lulac, Grey					43	43	46	57	80	83	55	59
6281/75	Lulac, Grey								200	300	300	195	211
6282/25	Lulac, Beige					43	43	46	57	80	83	55	59
6282/75	Lulac, Brown								200	300	300	300	324
6283/50	Lulac, Brown				72	72	72	76	92	130	135	86	93
6284/60	Dangling Dog	105	115									185	204
6284/99	Lulac, Cream										575	575	621
6285/55	Lulac Tiger			125	125	125	125					235	254
6285/60	Dangling Tomcat	105										185	204
6287/70	Dangling Dog											220	233
6288/32	Dangling Monkey "Mungo"							60	72			110	119
6290/32	Dangling Cat "Burri"							60	72	110		110	119
6291/32	Dangling Dog "Lumpi"							60	72	110		110	119
6292/32	Dangling Frog "Cappy"							60	72	110		110	119
6294/32	Dangling Mouse "Pieps"							60	72			110	119
6304/50	Hippo	170										300	330
6305/50	Rhino	170										300	330
6310/60	Bison	175	195	200	200	200						325	358
6314/60	Tiger	138	150	155	155							270	297
6315/30	Puma, Lying	75	75									145	155
6315/40	Puma, Standing	80	87									155	175
6315/99	Puma, Lying	375		425	425	425						750	850
6316/99	Puma, Sitting	590		700	700	700						1100	1300
6320/30	Leopard, Lying	75	82									145	155
6320/40	Leopard, Standing	80	80									155	175
6320/99	Leopard, Lying	375	415	425	425	425	425					750	800
6321/99	Leopard, Standing	590	650	675	675	675	675					1100	1300
6322/99	Leopard, Sitting St	695	713	700	700	700	700					1300	1400
6323/99	Panther, Lying	375	415	425	425	425						750	850
6325/99	Panther, Standing	590	650	675	675	675						1100	1300
6360/12	Teddy Shoulder Bag	10	11	12	12							22	33
6361/12	Teddy Coin Purse	10	11	12								22	33
6365/26	Teddy Shoulder Bag, Lg.	17	19	19	19							34	45
6370/22	Bear Music Box	49	54	54	54	54	54	54				97	99
6371/22	Cat Music Box	49										97	99
6376/18	Owl Music Box	44	48	49	49							88	95
6383/18	Ladybug Music Box	26	30									59	64
6400/15	Mosaic Ball, Sm., mhr	17	21	22								65	69
6400/20	Mosaic Ball, Med., mhr	28	32	32								110	115
6422/24	Donkey Pull Toy			62								115	120
6450/15	Ball				21	21	21	22	27	42		45	49
6450/20	Ball				32	32	32	34	41	65		69	75
6460/27	Chimpanzee (Hand Puppet)	26	28	28	28	28	28	30	36			50	56
6461/27	Bear (Hand Puppet)	26	28	28	28	28	28	30	36			60	67
6462/27	Frog (Hand Puppet)	26	28									50	56
6463/27	Rabbit (Hand Puppet)	30	33	33	33	33	33	35	42			55	62
6464/27	Dog (Hand Puppet)	30	32									55	62
6466/27	Cat (Hand Puppet)	30	33	33	33							55	62
6470/27	Owl (Hand Puppet)	30	33									55	62
6471/27	Lion (Hand Puppet)	33	36	37	37	37	37	39	47			62	69
6472/27	Fox (Hand Puppet)	33	36									62	69
6474/27	Wolf (Hand Puppet)	33	36									62	69
6476/27	Crocodile (Hand Puppet)	33	36									62	69
6485/32	Happy Bear										95	95	103
6488/32	Happy Guenon Monkey										105	105	113
6490/32	Happy Rabbit										105	105	113
6494/32	Happy Cat										115	115	124
6496/32	Happy Hedgehog										95	95	103
6497/32	Happy Fox										115	115	124
651847	Petsile, The Toy Store, 1993, LE 1500 announced, 950 produced												150

Steiff #	Description	80-81	81-82	82-83	83-84	84-85	85-86	86	87	88	89	90	Current
6560/17	Teddy (Hand Puppet), mhr	19										110	123
6600/17	Rabbit (Hand Puppet), mhr	20										85	95
6640/17	Fox Terrier (Hand Puppet), mhr	20										85	95
6660/17	Cat, Grey (Hand Puppet), mhr	20										85	95
6820/18	Lion (Hand Puppet), mhr	23										90	101
6880/17	Tiger (Hand Puppet), mhr	23										90	101
6991/30	Chimpanzee (Hand Puppet)	46	50	51	51	51	51	54	65			85	95
6992/30	Bear (Hand Puppet)	46	50	51	51	51	51	54	65			85	95
6993/30	Rabbit (Hand Puppet)	46	50	51	51	51	51	54	65			85	95
6994/30	Dog (Hand Puppet)	46	50									85	95
6995/30	Owl (Hand Puppet)	50	55									85	95
6996/30	Donkey (Hand Puppet)	46										85	95
6998/30	Cat	46	50									85	95
7010/45	Grey Jolly Rabbit Elbow Puppet									170		175	189
7086/10	Wool Bird Assmt	10	10									16	18
7116/08	Birds, Assmt	5	7	7	7							11	12
7136/04	Rabbits, Assmt	5	7	7	7	7						11	12
7146/06	Rabbits, Assmt	8	10	10	10	10	10	10	12			15	17
7156/08	Rabbits, Assmt	13	15	15	15	15	15	16	20			22	24
7170/06	Guniea Pig	9	9									15	17
7173/06	Hampster	8	8									12	13
7180/05	Frog	7	8	8	8							14	15
7180/07	Frog	8	10	10	10							16	18
7212/08	Duckling	9	10									14	15
7240/08	Rooster	7	8	8								11	12
7245/08	Rooster	9	11	11	11							16	18
7250/08	Hen	7	8	8								11	12
7255/08	Hen	9	11	11	11	11						16	18
7260/04	Chick	4	5	6	6							8	9
7260/06	Chick	5	7	7	7	7						10	11
7260/08	Chick	9	11	11	11							16	18
7276/09	Fish, Assmt	10	11									19	21
7354/04	Mouse, White	5	7	7	7							9	10
7355/04	Mouse, Grey	5	7	7	7							9	10
7370/03	Lady Bug	5	6	7								9	10
7370/04	Lady Bug	4	5	5	6							7	8
7370/06	Lady Bug	5	7	7	8							9	10
7390/10	Penquin	8	10									15	17
7480/06	Owl	7	9	9	9							12	13
7480/09	Owl	9	11	11	11							16	18
7492/05	Pitty Bear	6	7									15	17
7493/05	Pitty Fox	6	7									9	10
7494/05	Pitty Cat	6	7									9	10
7495/05	Pitty Rabbit	6	7			7	7	7				10	11
7496/05	Pitty Lamb	6	7									9	10
7497/05	Pitty Dog	6	7									9	10
7500/05	Pitty Elephant	6	7									9	10
7501/05	Pitty Lion	6	7									9	10
7502/05	Pitty Squirrel	6	7									9	10
7503/05	Pitty Mice	8	9									14	15
7580/27	Toldi Bear SOS										82	82	89
7627/12	Boy Mecki Character	13	16	17	18	20	20	21	27	45	45	45	49
7627/17	Man Mecki Character	32	39	39	41	50	50	53	65	95	95	95	99
7627/28	Man Mecki Character	410	60	61	65	70	70	75	90	145	145	145	155
7627/50	Mecki, Man			180	195	195	195					340	355
7628/12	Girl Mecki Character	13	16	17	18	20	20	21	27	45	45	45	49
7628/17	Woman Mecki Character	32	39	39	41	50	50	53	65	95	95	95	99
7628/28	Woman Mecki Character	410	60	61	65	70	70	75	90	145	145	145	155
7628/50	Mecki, Woman			180	195	195	195					340	355
7635/19	Santa Claus, LE 2000-1985						75	75	75			125	138
7635/28	Santa Claus, LE 1200-1984/2000-1985					95	95	100	100			155	171
7690/20	Shepard	31	34									60	69
7851/25	Doll, Madi			36								65	70
7860/20	Bambi Fawn					34	34	36				75	95
7871/28	Doll, Marion			43	43							80	86
7872/28	Doll, Marc			43	43							80	86
7873/28	Doll, Tanja			43	43							80	86
7874/28	Doll, Michael			43								80	86
7875/28	Doll, Yvonne			43								80	86

Numerical Listing

Steiff #	Description	80-81	81-82	82-83	83-84	84-85	85-86	86	87	88	89	90	Current
7892/40	Doll, Punch			56								100	108
8010/40	Riding Bear	185										355	367
8020/45	Rocking Duck	150										295	310
8130/50	Riding Animal, Rocking Bear			285	295	295	295	310	375	600	600	385	416
8135/50	Riding Animal, Rocking Pony			285	295	295	295	310	375	600	600	385	416
8150/40	Riding Animal, Riding Bear Rocker	205	210	215	285	285	300					395	400
8155/50	Riding Animal, Bear on Wheels	285	290	295								565	575
8175/60	Riding Animal, Pony on Wheels	295	300	300								570	585
8190/30	Riding Animal, Ladybug/Wheels	185	190	195	195	195	205	250	375			350	375
8195/45	Riding Animal, Rocking Duck	175	180	175	175	175						330	350
8452/22	Broken Set Nimrod Bear, Caramel, LE					45						100	109
8453/22	Broken Set Nimrod Bear, White, LE					45	35					96	109
8455/22	Broken Set Nimrod Bear, Brass, LE					45						100	109
8470/17	Teeny Teddy Bag							60	77			80	86
8472/17	Teeny Bag Panda							60	55			60	65
8474/17	Teeny Bag Rabbit							60	55			60	65
8476/17	Teeny Bag Dog							60	55			60	65
8490/12	Teddy Minibag				12	12	12	15	22	22		23	24
8492/26	Teddy Bag				19	19	20	24	35			37	39
8494/03	Teddy Pin with Ribbon, mhr							20	19	19		22	30
8495/03	Teddy Pin, Beige, mhr				17	18	19	19				24	26
8496/03	Teddy Pin, Caramel, mhr				17	18	19	19				24	26
8497/03	Teddy Pin, White, mhr				17	18	19	19		19		24	26
8498/03	Teddy Pin, Chocolate, mhr				17	18	19	19		19		24	26
8500/03	Teddy Bear Pin				9	9	10	12		12		14	15
8501/02	Gold Plated Bar Pin w/Jointed Bear						15	18		27		22	29
8505/01	Gold Plated Teddy Earrings			20		21	27			46	46	46	50
8510/02	Gold Plated Teddy Necklace				15	15	16	20		32	32	210	32
8550/02	Reg Edition, History of Steiff										100	100	120
8601/06	Porcelain Tea Set, 7 pc.									18	15	20	29
8605/01	Wall Plate										9	9	10
8605/06	Mini Tea Set										15	15	16
8605/15	Deluxe Tea Set										57	57	62

Special Editions by Hobby Center Toys and The Toy Store. (Left to Right) Mr. Vanilla, 0152/25cm, 1989 (HCT), $335; Panda, 0218/14cm, 1988 (HCT), $350; Teddy Bear Baby Rose, 1990 (HCT); Dicky Mauve, 0172/18, 1991 (HCT), $275; Dicky Rose, 0179/19, 1990 (HCT) $350; Teddile, 011979, 1992 (TS), $125; Petsile, 651847, 25cm, 1993 (TS), $150.
Photography by Dick Frantz.

Special Acknowledgments

Many companies and individuals have helped with the compilation of this book.

Dick Frantz

Margarete Steiff GmbH

Reeves International, Inc.

Cynthia Britnall of Cynthia's Country Store,
11496 Pierson Road, #C-1, Commerce Park,
Wellington, West Palm Beach, FL 33414
(407) 793-0554.

Color Collector's Catalogue and Newsletter/Price Guide — $16.00 year

0111,35
Lion

0111,22
Lion

Lion, Lying, 0111/35,
L.E. 1000, 1984, $294.
*Photograph courtesy of
Margarete Steiff GmbH and
Reeves International.*

Steiff Reference Books

Consult your favorite merchant or call Hobby House Press, toll-free at **1-800-554-1447**.

Steiff: Sensational Teddy Bears, Animals & Dolls
by Christel & Rolf Pistorius
Experience the endearing charm of Steiff's teddy bears and a bevy
of Steiff animals in this richly illustrated, large format photograph
album showcasing 100 years of the renowned German company. This
book has significant coverage on post WWII Steiff which is in such
demand by collectors. Compiled and illustrated by animal type thus
enhancing its usability. Certainly the most beguiling, colorful story
of Steiff teddy bears and animals, with 258 color photographs out of
288 photographs. 160 pages, 9" x 12-1/2". HB. Item #H3982. $39.95

4th Teddy Bear & friends® Price Guide
by Linda Mullins. Steiff Teddy Bears and other animals from antique right up to contemporary have significant coverage in this book.
Featured are the latest values on teddy bears, rabbits, cats and dogs
as well as a wealth of other animals. A large section is devoted to
such sought-after collectibles of Steiff (antique through museum &
limited editions), North American Bear (Muffy), Gund and wealth
of manufacturers and artists. Charts as well as 105 stunning color
and 259 b/w photographs capture the character of bears and their
friends. 192 pages. 6" x 9". PB. Item #H4438. $12.95